The Memphis Book

ISBN: 0-6157-4258-0
ISBN-13: 9780615742588

The Memphis Book

The story of a city: its history, its culture, its people and potential

Wesley Alan Wright

2013

Preface

Before I illuminate the details of what has been holding our city back and divulge the intricacies of my plans to help the city I wanted to share a letter just shared with citizens of Memphis as of January 2013 that validates and complements much of what I have been writing about and working so hard for four years interviewing and gathering information to solve issues that I have longed to tackle as a Memphis citizen, block club captain, leader in the Vollintine Evergreen Neighborhood and organizer of various community entities. I was frankly tired of seeing little action from city leaders that suggest conscious planning. Here is that letter that confirmed I was not alone:

Dear Fellow Memphians:
Our city is at a crossroads. Steadily, we are losing population and businesses because crime is too high, public schools are struggling, and our property tax rate is higher than any other city in Tennessee.

In the areas of crime, education, and property taxes, our city needs dramatic change and we must do something within reason to stop the hemorrhaging. I'll explain:

1. Crime
Blue Crush is a program developed six years ago, which assigns police officers on "details" to areas of town hit hardest by crime based on data. From 2007 - 2011, the most serious crimes were reduced by 26.5%, due in part because we paid our police officers overtime to run Blue Crush details.

For some unknown reason, Blue Crush overtime was taken away from the Memphis Police Department in July 2011 without notice to the public, the Crime Commission, and the City Council.

As a result, Blue Crush details were reduced by 60 - 70% and serious crimes have increased in the last year by 10%.

For a detailed review of the changes made to Blue Crush, please see the three page summary I drafted and the documents I have uncovered in the last two months showing the cuts made to Blue Crush: See Blue Crush Analysis at http://www.cityofmemphis.org/Government/CityCouncil/District5.aspx

2. Education

Crime reduction, schools performance, and economic activity in Memphis would improve greatly over the long term if children entering kindergarten were better prepared for their education that follows. Recently, I was informed that a deal to bring a new company and jobs to Memphis fell apart due to the company's concerns over our public schools.

According to research done by the Urban Child Institute of Memphis, pre-Kindergarten programs for four-year-old children have resulted in significant improvements in cognitive and language skills, test scores, and motor skills. Children who have participated in pre-Kindergarten also have better attendance, fewer behavior problems, and increased chances of reading at grade level by the 4th grade. (See the Urban Child Institutes study at http://www.urbanchildinstitute.org/articles/policy-briefs).

If most grade school students in Memphis could read at grade level, we would see dramatic change in Memphis over the next 10 to 20 years. Children would be better educated and prepared for life after school and more would attend college. Crime and poverty would go down. Memphis would be better prepared to recruit businesses and jobs to the city.

3. Property Taxes

For years, Memphis has been saddled with the State's highest combined property tax rate (county and city). We currently pay 40% more than the citizens of Chattanooga and 53% more than the taxpayers of Nashville.

Differences in our property tax rate and those in other cities result in "hundreds of thousands of dollars" in additional taxes to be paid by potential investors if they come to Memphis. Our relatively high rate is "driving investment out of the city." (Memphis Business Journal, April 27, 2012).

The City Council has cut the property tax rate from 3.43 to 3.11 in the last four years. We need to push it down even further to be competitive.

4. Proposed Solutions

With respect to crime reduction, we need the Mayor and the Memphis Police Department to commit to once again fully funding and implementing Blue Crush. I will ask for such commitments.

During the five years I have served on your Memphis City Council, I have never supported a tax increase, particularly because the revenue was destined for the city's operating budget to be used in a non-specific way.

Several years ago, I heard then-Governor Phil Bredesen reflect on his time as mayor of Nashville. He said that government never should ask for a tax increase simply to pay its ordinary operating expenses, and I agree with him. Any tax increase should be used for new programs and be clearly defined. Taxpayers should always be allowed to vote any tax increase up or down.

Currently, along with Councilman Shea Flinn, I am proposing a public referendum to increase the city's sales tax by one-half (0.5) percent from 9.25% to 9.75%. It is estimated that such increase would result in $47 million in revenue.

We also propose a commitment to spend this income as follows: $27 million for the pre-Kindergarten education of 4 year old children in Memphis and $20 million to reduce the city's property tax rate by 20 cents from 3.11 to 2.91. (That would result in an overall 15% reduction from the 3.43 rate we had five years ago).

We need to drastically reduce crime and our property tax rate and improve education if this city has a chance. This sales tax proposal helps us with all three of these issues.

We have cut the property tax rate in the last four years and I will continue to lead the push to lower expenses and property taxes. As Memphis Magazine points out, "Strickland has evolved into the council's most persistent voice for greater budgetary discipline." (August 2010).

This is a game changer for Memphis. We are often only given one opportunity to make dramatic change for our community, and I am hopeful that our city will come together and grab this chance for substantial improvement.

If you have any questions or concerns about these issues, or any other issues, please let me know.

Sincerely,
Jim Strickland

I applaud the words of Councilman Jim Strickland who apparently has a fresh and discerning grasp of the situation. However he is not fully aware of the grand scheme in education as I have a book out entitled *The Education Artifice* that will flesh out the problems with the Pre-K program. Jim Strickland has all of his ideas well envisioned except the pre-Kindergarten education concept, although more can be said of other problems later let's stay on course. The Urban Child Institute of Memphis has conducted studies as if in a vacuum that will in the long run change course unbeknownst to them because of a myriad of factors. Some of those factors involve post elementary weaknesses in middle school and high school structuring, curriculum and administrative management that is not conducive to college preparatory standards nationwide. Those are just scratching the surface. Consequently he made a point to get more kids in college, that is not what is needed, but that we give them a chance to succeed in college is more important. Far too many children will enter college and fall out the first or second semester. Diplomas and college entrance should not be a measuring stick. Yes, please lay that foundation for the 3 and 4 year old children, what the studies contend about cognitive and language skills, test scores, and motor skills are accurate. However, Memphis City Schools is not prepared to usher in the pre-K program children and carry the torch to the finish line or for that matter into middle school. The weakest link where trench warfare for the future of our youth is in middle school, fix the whole railway not just the train station.

This is not an attack on the teachers, it is the system that envelopes the teachers that has failed. It is not just a matter of establishing this program citywide should it be approved by a poorly performing cognitively narrow leadership, but that the school system itself needs a comprehensive overhaul that will deconstruct the weaknesses of urban traditional public education K- 12 and act upon it. Otherwise we are giving a facelift to a decaying structure built on a sandbar. *The Education Artifice* elucidates just that, no shame in plugging my book here since I did not want to make a 500 page book combining Memphis and Education. Consider them linked since education is the most important leg in the tripod of education, commerce and transportation that I will speak of throughout this book. Once again, I want to commend Councilman Jim Strickland and Shea Flinn for their fiscally responsible and big picture thinking, their proposition will have more benefits than any suggestions I have yet to see. I have several friends who are in appointed positions in city and county capacities, but to no avail have I been able to get the point across, hence this book and the hopeful movement to ensue. The last chapter will coincide with many of the ideas leadership should embrace if they have not already done so. This is not a static monologue but hopefully a dynamic dialogue whereby channels of constructive discourse will ensue and expound upon what is in this book, whether agreeing or disagreeing it is good to move forward with big picture thinking.

I am putting forth a daring discourse and perhaps considered suicidal by some of my peers, it is also pertinent for you to fully envelope the ideas in this book before making a complete judgment on the work itself. It is with this integral thought in which the ideas in this book pivot and on this concept we traverse diverse subject matters. Consequently, it is also important to know that this book is a collection of ideas over time, beyond four years and with its colorful nomenclature will be honest. The ideas put forth are a collection of many impromptu interviews and discussions of which were sincere, anonymous and relevant to the whole concept of the book. I say this because two chapters in particular highlight the views of many of my interviewees and as such I am simply a sounding board and not the orator. This book will be holistic in its approach to solving the problems of Memphis while also embracing its myriad of strengths, and then, moving forward with that understanding. Make sure not to read snippets or you could otherwise get the wrong idea altogether. No person associated with me either through social media, church or schools were interviewed and so should not be considered as any of the "anonymous" people I used for their perspectives.

The use of data may come to question, for empirical and academic uses by some readers. It is widely known in the world of academia that all books written from Harvard professors to community college graduate students to random authors have the stain of subjectivity and as such have and will use data to their purpose. So, I use all data with caution, I do not dismiss it, but I take into consideration how it can be manipulated. I gathered data from sources at street level to respected texts that from some of which you will see quotes before each chapter. Many areas from transportation to education where an analysis is made I had the input and support of professionals and their praise in trying to tie in all of the many varied subjects. There is no bibliography or data charts due to the tremendous length it would add to this book and the unapproachable timbre it would instill in this book. Consequently, much of the information used to construct this book is Memphis specific and as such is original and my interviews are the source since no book of this type has ever been written so there are not many books I could draw from. I believe my book is very informative. I had an invigorating discussion via Delta Does Memphis before re-releasing this book that shed light on several things. One, if my book appears in any way to slander the leadership of Memphis then I am considered a target or threat. Two, the people whose job I may seem to be questioning will then in turn come after me and my credentials. Three, the people who have approached me via Facebook, Twitter, email or in person who have criticized my book even though none of them have admitted to reading it, most of them work directly with, for or under Mayor Wharton or an elected official. Four, people with a conflict of interest who are essentially defending their paycheck by attacking me need to inbox me privately since their intentions and objectivity might get hazy regardless of degrees or positions and thus nullifying objectivity. Five, read the book in its entirely as it states in the premise before you criticize the academia or validity of the findings. Six, consequently, I do not attack Mayor Wharton in the book, I speak highly of his efforts. Seven, I stopped posting via Facebook with much frequency because I feel it is not a platform conducive to serious discussion nor taken seriously by supporters or critics. What I have gathered from the first release is that this text in some parts will preach to the choir, in others it may step on toes.

The intellectual elite that will more often attack this book do so because they have had no success themselves in drawing a balanced picture of the dismal state of Memphis and the silver lining. This book and my background fly in the face of the old school adage of publishing and academia though I have three college degrees since I am not an anointed as a professor or informed government contractor. I do not claim expertise here, but valuable information, professional analysis and rigorous research. Most who will criticize my findings are likened to film critics who could never make a movie and as such are bitter. Another commonality of my critics is that they are far removed from the reality of Memphis because their kids if they have any are in private schools, or they live in affluent enclaves, or they are imports who came here for government work, corporate work or otherwise and have not absorbed the truth. Most who get mired in the data and do not offer comprehensive solutions attack this book because if they offered the same honesty in a book of their own they would be biting the hand that feeds them and get fired. Essentially, talk is what you will get from most of these pundits and not action even in the form of a book. So, my answer to them is, please, write your own book and then come back to me, if you have insights or suggestions write me at Wesley@wesleyalanwright.com. Please read the text around the images (in the middle of the book) since much of it is perhaps the most important data you will see in the book. Consequently this book has a frank assessment of Memphis past, present and possible future and it's not structured so rigid academically that it is inaccessible. However, if its gets too heavy, put it down and continue later, but don't put it away.

chapter I

Beginnings

What we call the beginning is often the end. And to make an end
is to make a beginning. The end is where we start from.
~ T. S. Eliot

It's a lovely evening, it's just around sunset, and I am with my wife of almost three years by the waters of the mighty Mississippi. It feels oddly comfortable for an August evening, a nice breeze in the air, no mosquitoes, families and couples walk by as we sit on a bench. I noticed a certain anonymity or benign presence about us being there—it was pleasant. It was not yet completely dark, the sun still fading and the lights began to come on to illuminate the walkways that were just in front of us as we sat on a park bench. I thought quietly to myself, this is not Memphis! I can hear myself think, no loud music resonating from a souped-up car. It's almost like everyone is colorblind, nobody looks around with leery eyes. Memphis has a lot of green spaces and is very in touch with nature, but I haven't noticed any graffiti or damage to the park. Just when I am on cloud nine, I look back and notice that some people in the parking lot in the distance are just sitting in their cars observing with some loud rap song echoing off the bluffs just yards away—so much for enjoying nature. Ahhh, Memphis, you're back.

My little daughter was at home, I then thought maybe that was a good idea. I notice that my wife and I start to get strange looks, and I thought, is it that I am just being hypersensitive? It's the city, you are supposed to have noise, that's what makes the phrase the city that never sleeps work. Memphis is by no means New York City, but it has its own claims to fame—that I will delve into later. I am tired of people giving me that look, rolling around in their tinted window cars, playing repetitious music that doesn't even visit the treble clef. Memphis, what's the deal? Well, I asked my wife about it and she said, "babe, I'm black, you are white, this is normal here." Yeah, I know, but I was starting to enjoy my evening not being reminded that I live in such a racist town. We get that "what are you two doing together?" look all the time here in Memphis, from all colors. I cannot say I have experienced that same feeling or stare anywhere else in the United States, or overseas for that matter. Why is that?

While you were reading did you see that coming? What did you honestly think my shade of skin was going to be? I am a mutt of Cherokee, Jewish, Welsh, and English, but I am white—that's ok, let's just call a spade a spade. Memphis is comprised of a multitude of ethnicities but not pre-dominantly international in the non-Anglo Saxon sense. My wife is from Kenya, I have dated numerous African American women but that doesn't matter, I am still some kind of racist, right? My students in middle school take it that I am a bigot of sorts because I am hard on them and don't have street dialect as they would describe it, so, obviously, I am a racist. Funny though when the school counselor mentions my wife, theories seem to change—I don't have a clan suit back at home after all. That would be silly wouldn't it, to be married to a black woman and teach in a school that's 99% African American, wouldn't I just loose my mind?

I haven't, nor will I drop the N word in this book, or in person. It doesn't belong in anyone's lexicon, but people still give power to it through comedy and music and other mediums. It's a one way street though, a double standard that whites cannot say it, but blacks can. Funny those blacks can use "cracker" or "cracka" in dialogue and it just be humor. Asian comics sling their rhetoric pretty loosely too, but Caucasians have to walk gently don't they? DL Hughley spoke on CNN last night about the need for honest dialogue between groups about how we truly feel. I agreed whole heartedly with him. Soledad Obrien who is a reporter for CNN often speaks with ease around the color line because of her ethnic backgrounds, which the last name might reveal some. She has shed light on realities through documentary style productions concerning New Orleans (2010) and Black in America 1 and 2 (2008, 2009). Obrien illustrates realities about the human condition such as race and identity, poverty, education and other issues which are interwoven and should not be discussed as exclusive. Local News affiliates have produced series after series that address the tensions that are very apparent in the mid-south (the region where Mississippi, Tennessee and Arkansas meet) between white and blacks and how they manifest and how one could deal with them. Michael Eric Dyson, famous for his eloquence and introspective discourse has been on numerous shows, written books and has been an asset to the African American movement. Bill Cosby has also put in his two cents.

All of these efforts are commendable and worthy of observation and reflection. However, one common denominator amongst all of the aforementioned scholars, entertainers and reporters—they are not white. With respect, very little has been written about the Caucasian experience in the 21st century along the lines of race. This is not to say that whites have suffered onslaughts of racism and that they too should demand an audience. What I want to bring to light is the underlying theme that gets grazed by African Americans through various mediums and one that Caucasians are often too afraid to address for fears of being ostracized or destroying a possible career. I want to illuminate what whites have been thinking the last twenty years in one city known for rock and roll, the home of the blues, where King was assassinated and where people visit and have mixed experiences, no pun intended. I want to address this book primarily to the readers out there of European descent and question them, what are you doing about this? As for African Americans, this would be a great read to see into the minds of whites, whom some of them you work with, go to church with, see at a restaurant or have sex with. Most African Americans really don't know what whites are thinking, and most whites aren't really honest with themselves and by extension act irrationally in regards to race. This is a two way street of racial but more often cultural and socio-economic discord that traverses across color boundaries and permeates almost every aspect of our livelihood. In Memphis, where this is most impactful is not just tension, but commercial growth, neighborhood stability, quality of Education and so many other aspects that I have linked as part of the same ecosystem. I discussed *The Memphis Book* with many people and at first it seemed like a novel concept but once they grasped core themes in this book it was very important to them that it be addressed on a city-wide and perhaps nationwide scale openly.

I want to stress, I have not come upon this topic abruptly and have not done so to incite hatred or division but rather to expose the division that is most evident in my eyes and that which is suppressed for the sake of comfort or political correctness. I want to also clarify that I use black and African American interchangeably as do I with white and Caucasian. Whichever word fits my idea or was used by my interviewees at the time will be used, but they have the same meaning. Without connecting or finding reasonable coexistence between our diverse societies the United States will fall from within. I am not suggesting that large-scale race riots will bring impending doom—those are hiccups which come and go on and off the proverbial radar. What I am suggesting is that our dysfunction as a nation are on matters purely superficial but also conversely complex as race has and will make matters worse and cripple the systems of law enforcement, education and even capitalism itself. The writing is on the wall: Mene, Mene, Tekel, Parsin—much the same way Rome and Babylon fell, America is fat with contentment in its illusions of wealth, prosperity, and supremacy and will falter internally of strife, one of them being racial discord. So, it should be said, the subtle effects of bigotry on society and those more obvious are all-encompassing and should be acknowledged before the greatness that is the United States should end. Bigotry, one should note, can manifest itself in terms of socio-economics, culture or ethnicity or other ways. All great nations pass, empires last but an average of 400 years—but as the world around America changes and the United States puts on blinders, our country will only decay more and more, only to the surprise of most when it's too late and the damage has been done. So, I want this book to be a catalyst for discussion and healing—and furthermost introspection, looking within, for which ultimately must require accountability from all of us, regardless of creed or race.

It should be said that it is right to judge and mold perceptions—for if something is neither reflected nor judged is it desirable that we should acknowledge its existence? For without day, or the naming of day, there is no darkness, one must distinguish, without compensation for winner and looser how is it competition and what would be the purpose of sport? Such it is in life that we form thoughts that we may advance thought; though some may not glean truth or righteous views from it. Perceptions are often misguided, although some use factual scrutiny and are not completely unfounded. So it is alarming and perhaps dangerous that we draw lines in the sand to divide ourselves from others, to form ethical boundaries, religious margins while the tide of life often erases or shallows those lines. Experiences are those tides, the lines are our tenets, the perceptions are what occurs because of the tide, and what stands on the other side of that line we have drawn. Stereotypes stem from perceptions that are misleading, but should some things that are true though unpopular be kept quiet? Such as it is within society we view people, color and "race" with varied stances depending on our genesis and our journey since then. I hope I didn't lose anyone there, but if so, read that again. Essentially I am saying that this discord whether racial, ethnic or cultural has socio-economic repercussions and politically corrosive traits on a national scale that have not been fully understood or discovered by academics.

Let me briefly digress so that we can find the parallels concerning perception and reality and how we live because of it. Since I started writing this book one great event in race relations as it has been proclaimed has occurred. The United States elected and swore in its first African American president in 2008 opening a new dawn of freedom and opportunity for people of color. That last sentence is riddled with problems; much like a minefield coats a Middle Eastern countryside with danger. The greatest misconception is that being 1% black makes you black as the popular maxim states. Another misconception is that electing a black president shows that America is opening up and walls of oppression have been knocked down. Sure, there has been some progress but it is a gradual process and often what could be seen as progress is a façade. You may ask, where is he going with this? Is he trying to open old wounds? What I am asserting is that those wounds are still present and media, pop culture, academics and others have fallen for the same serenade of false impressions that inhabit throngs of hopeful people.

One's view of the president often is not molded from facts but from perceptions ingrained from partisan sentiments, media induced or rather intravenously with ones upbringing. Ideologies associated with that president whether through his party or random statements (i.e. sound bites) from the man himself hold sway to our allegiance regardless of specifics concerning what is really at stake and what should be done. Objectivity is lost in our dogmatic bombast to push our agenda rather than seek sensible resolutions. This is sad, though most of America sees partisanship as elemental and necessary. I say that last sentence even though now with the fiscal cliff of 2013 awaiting us, people are tired of partisan pettiness, but they still elected a majority of the same politicians back, that doesn't add up does it? Ultimately this will lead to the folly of our society. You may ask, how can this be, we have survived this long? Survived is the key word, not thrived—only in several segments of our history have we been envied by the world, if that. Partisanship is deep seeded and second nature to United States policy and decisions made by government and its three branches on federal and local levels. Party supporters follow suit as a dog with his master or a flock with its shepherd—hardly conscientious. In the late 18th century the original design by Jefferson and many of the founding council did not desire a party based government, though they feared its inevitability. Washington spoke vehemently against partisanship in his farewell speech saying it would destroy our nation. It almost did in 1861.

Progress is unavoidably hindered through red tape and lobbying as well as machinery that compromises due process. In both Republican and Democratic parties there are men and women with genuine commitment to our country. They are however surrounded by a process that is anything but efficient and by people that see monetary gain and power with their positions. In the autumn of 2005 Hurricane Katrina stirred up some of these attitudes with regards to bureaucratic blundering by FEMA, but local democratically run parties as well. This is something that is noticed but not addressed enough and not discussed on a grand scale—it is simply headlined, exhausted but not resolved. There is neither ground broken nor any headway made when people do not step outside the box and see the forest for the trees. I want to introduce another issue, one with more history in view of world scope. From a local study of my own, government census and other parties in a southern town known for its tribulations we will try to tackle a delicate subject. Can one observe a race/ethnicity the same way? Well, people do. There is a correlation that is deeply troubling between perception and actuality and we will address it.

Along the great Mississippi, there is a growing metropolis known for its blues and gospel, home of the king of rock and roll, headquarters for FedEx and AutoZone and other national corporations. The land comprising present-day Memphis remained in a largely unorganized territory throughout most of the 18th century. In 1796, the site became the westernmost point of the newly admitted state of Tennessee, located in the Southwest United States. Memphis was founded in 1819 by John Overton, James Winchester and Andrew Jackson. Some of those names should be familiar to mid-Southerners and Americans in general. The city was named after the ancient capital of Egypt on the Nile River. Memphis developed as a transportation center in the 19th century because of its flood-free location, high above the Mississippi River. As the cotton economy of the antebellum South depended on the forced labor of large numbers of African-American slaves, Memphis became a major slave market. In 1857, the Memphis and Charleston Railroad was completed, the only east-west railroad across the southern states prior to the Civil War. Tennessee seceded from the Union in June 1861, and Memphis briefly became a Confederate stronghold. Union ironclad gunboats captured the city in the naval Battle of Memphis on June 6, 1862, and the city remained under Union control for the duration of the war. Memphis became a Union supply base and continued to prosper throughout the war. Meanwhile, Confederate General Nathan Bedford Forrest harassed Union forces in the area.

In the 1870s, a series of yellow fever epidemics devastated Memphis. The worst outbreak, in 1878, reduced the population by nearly 75% as many people died or fled the city permanently. Property tax revenues collapsed, and the city could not make payments on its municipal debts. As a result, Memphis temporarily lost its city charter and was a taxing district from 1878–1893. The city regained its charter in 1893. Memphis grew into the world's largest spot cotton market and the world's largest hardwood lumber market.

From the 1910s to the 1950s, Memphis was a place of machine politics under the direction of E. H. "Boss" Crump. During the Crump era, Memphis developed an extensive network of parks and public works as part of the National City Beautiful movement. Determined never to suffer plagues again, it rebuilt with meticulous sanitation and drainage. However, it did not encourage heavy industry and Mr. Crump's heavy arm outstretched too far and banned movies alienated Memphis politically, commercially and by extension socio-economically. During the 1960s, the city was at the center of civil rights issues, notably a sanitation workers' strike. The Lorraine Motel in the city was also the venue of the assassination of Martin Luther King, Jr. on April 4, 1968, the day after giving his prophetic I've Been to the Mountaintop speech at the Mason Temple. In 1970, the Census Bureau reported Memphis' population as 60.8% white and 38.9% black. That has shifted like a mirror image in present day Memphis where it's currently 61% African American, 34% Caucasian and the remainder other ethnic groups. That rapid change caused migration unlike many large cities who had already absorbed integration, however this may not just be unique to Memphis and so this book should be a framework study and hopeful catalyst for positive change.

Memphis is well known for its cultural contributions to the identity of the American South. Many renowned musicians grew up in and around Memphis and moved from the Mississippi Delta. Just in the last 10 years Memphis has experienced a downtown renaissance, some would date it earlier in the mid-1990s. This town has historically experienced hardships such as POST Civil War Reconstruction, the Yellow Fever breakouts in the later 19th century, and financial ruin during the Great Depression. More recently the Civil Rights turbulence that included the death of Dr. Martin Luther King is foremost in the psyche of Americans all over the country. Memphis is a resilient town, though the same can be said for many southern towns such as Atlanta and Charleston who experience far worse during the Civil War. It is a wonderful city with diverse cultures and traditions so as to form a mosaic. However, a melting pot this "city on the bluff" it is not, only in patches and circles like the churches or the arts do you see cohabitation and collaboration across ethnic/cultural boundaries. There are always exceptions to this, considering rock and roll was a merging of African styles emanating from blues and gospel and from a variety of classical styles in white music. Rock was born in Memphis, but this attitude of collaboration did not carry throughout the city. Memphis also has a strong tone of piety and known for its churches of all colors. One cannot say with assurance this is a Memphis problem or an aberration, but before I say this is rampant everywhere we should let the elements here in Memphis speak for themselves and readers elsewhere can make assessments of their own fair city or town.

In today's world of political correctness we find ourselves afraid or oblivious of forthright statements, which in many cases may seem bigoted or ignorant. We all come from something; this is painfully true in American society—especially in urban areas. There are schisms in Memphis where tension grows ever so subtle and people on both sides whether black or white, Chinese or black or other have a mutual contempt for each other. Some of this hostility is perhaps substantiated yet for most citizens baseless. These tensions manifest themselves violently ever so often and yet most of the times are commonplace nuances in our daily behavior. For example in Memphis, there lie severe disparities that smack of caste systemization in shopping malls where most people beneath the surface have apprehensive feelings about other ethnicities. This is especially true between men and women of African descent and those of European descent. This is a rift that has not been mended yet most people on both sides assume it's there, deal with it; it won't do any more harm than it already has. These are strong words, but for something to be restored (although restore for Memphis could not apply because there has always been distinction and thus tension since post-Civil War) or remedied it must first be acknowledged. In Memphis, it is simply commonplace and hushed or eschewed. Where am I going with this? I want to be transparent, that currently the financial infrastructure and overall well-being of Memphis has suffered because of this and will hold the city back. Let us first address the word: race.

Racism is a problematic term in its root because it is contradictory in its definitive nature. Race is defined as thus: one of the major zoological subdivisions of mankind, regarded as having a common origin and exhibiting a relatively constant set of physical traits, such as pigmentation, hair form, and facial and bodily proportions—or assumed to have, common characteristics, habits, appearances etc.; also any class of beings having characteristics uniting them, or differentiating them from others. Notice that, it does indeed acknowledge that in the separation of races, they are all granted impartiality, being deemed as partly man. Human is defined: having the nature or attributes of man; consisting of a man or men: human race. Also, ethnic is defined: Of, belonging to, or distinctive of a particular racial, cultural, or language division of mankind. Man is defined: Human beings collectively; the human race; mankind. In the end, dictionaries today state all three groups (Negroid, Mongoloid and Caucasoid) as being of mankind—the same cannot be said of the mindset centuries before Noah Webster. The separation is physically determined, not concerning intelligence, culture or otherwise—take note ethnicity is as a subgroup of race, though race is also defined as mankind as a whole. Anthropology and most religions have established that there is only one race, and that is the human race, how can one be racist? That is to say that they hate themselves? To differentiate colors or descent it is better to use in anthropological terms the word ethnicity. Sadly "ethnically biased" or prejudicial does sound politically correct but in this case it is the correct way of saying you hate a group of people. Political correctness is something that has gotten out of hand in our society where we water-down our problems with semantically apropos words and phrases so as not to offend anyone.

This is where I must traverse; into dangerous waters where some people could be offended in order to establish and solidify factual truths or simple realities and perceptions and make any headway concerning matters of ethnic/cultural friction that plague American society or Memphis at least. We will look at the city's demographic state, a certain shopping area where the neighborhoods converge, other issues, my personal experiences and good things Memphis can do to rise above the problems that hold our city back from greater things.

chapter II

The city's demographic reality

There are lies, damn lies and statistics. – Mark Twain

Facts are stubborn things, but statistics are more pliable.
~ Author Unknown

While the individual man is an insoluble puzzle, in the aggregate he becomes a mathematical certainty. You can, for example, never foretell what any one man will be up to, but you can say with precision what an average number will be up to. Individuals vary, but percentages remain constant. So says the statistician. ~ Arthur Conan Doyle

Torture numbers, and they'll confess to anything. ~ Gregg Easterbrook

The city of Memphis has a term that has gained popularity from those who have tried to escape its less becoming areas. As said previously, Memphis is a mosaic and not a melting pot with exceptions in a few neighborhoods. Hence the segmentation, the provincial neighborhood don't get out of mentality, hence the blight flight when a neighborhood goes down, hence the commercial struggle and school system decay. If I seem to be redundant it is because it's intentional and I want there to be an undercurrent of this logic throughout. There is a term perhaps of condescension or bigotry, but what it cannot be is one of endearment or admiration. In case you may not have guessed: Memphrika, because it is slang it could be spelled numerous other ways—though it's meaning is simple it can stir up many deep seeded emotions. When I was younger, my familiarity with the demographic landscape of inner Memphis led me to believe the United States to be more 50/50 in percentage to whites and blacks. I actually thought whites were possibly a minority. This was when I was young, much to my enlightenment as an adolescent in Political Science. Also, what I had learned was that Memphis was a poor city, underdeveloped, internally at odds, with less political influence than Nashville. It also had little to acclaim except Graceland, Beale Street and perhaps the Pink Palace. Presently, in retrospect, Memphis has come a long way in terms of becoming a tourist spot with more attractive sites, an expanded Zoo, countless museums (Children's Museum, Pink Palace Museum, Stax and more), and various federally and privately induced facelifts (i.e. Overton Park enhancements, Interstate 40 expansion, and the Bill Morris Parkway—soon to form a second loop around Memphis). The Sears Crosstown redevelopment project is impressive as well as the Overton Square renaissance. Our grand prize in the last fifteen years has been the FedEx Forum, though local government misappropriation and embezzlement in its construction has surfaced and scarred its short existence. Nevertheless, unless the segmentation is cured, these projects will be islands surrounded by blight and in the long term flashes in a pan. History will tell, but the past has already shown that these privately and publicly funded redevelopments are not sustainable unless the schools are performing well, the neighborhoods have citizens with jobs and a minimal flux of people are coming and going. The following chapters will elucidate these ideas.

Beginning in the late 1980s, the urban sprawl making rapid strides East and South and more recently in some sections north has been breaking records nationally. Towns like Collierville, Olive Branch and Southaven and Fayette County have absorbed much of the growing populace. Unfortunately our city's prosperous boom has been powered greatly by fears correlated or rather rooted in sentiments that do not reflect well on the image of Memphis. Midtown has remained a stronghold of relative tolerance and diversity where old money in pocketed enclaves, middle class white and black and small numbers of low income have subsisted for some time in close proximity. Midtown is almost an island, in every sense of the word, except that a large section to the east still remains predominantly white. However, practically in opposing fashion white middle class and up in the surrounding areas to the west, north and largely to the south have vacated further south or east in the last twenty years much to the detriment of city stability. Memphis is a financially unstable city but also in relations between ethnic groups, but they are interrelated. See, those two topics are married and most people leadership or otherwise don't get it or are too concerned about their career to address it openly and declaratively. The reputation of Memphis suffers because it reflects poorly on southern "backwardness" (i.e. appearing as if Jim Crow instigated zip code segregation) and ultimately national image which influences financial support on Federal, State and tourist influx. I have met many people who come to Memphis and their first impression was that it was like stepping back in time. Tourism is the biggest loser in this segmentation and backwardness. What I am saying may seem bigoted to some, but this is not a matter of opinion, it is an issue far too often silenced by political correctness. Though often-delayed, escapism comes at a price and the future of Memphis and possibly most American cities hinges on people of all colors to find some middle ground. I will elaborate why the very idea of suburbia is capitalistic and marketable but also infectious, comes with mixed motivations and often perilous outcomes if pushed too far and not exercised properly.

Many a movie, like *Pleasantville, American Beauty*, and the popular show *Desperate Housewives* displayed the caricatures both good and bad of suburbia. Stores such as Target (where I love to shop though I am a midtown-er), Pier I, Gap, Williams Sonoma and many others cater to the image often associated with upper crust living. This is not to say that only the wealthy can partake but it's the projection and shopping experience that speak in volumes. In the end, escapism (suburbia or within the I-240 loop) is key, not so much the package it comes in—for some their property spreads out like a ranch, for some a zero-lot house (which has become popular in interior Memphis, I will explain later how this is different) or for most others a development or community with a variety of houses with similar themes. People can live a life of serenity and peace, with isolation from the perilous world in the distance. Here their children can grow safely, with few visitors from the outside, a good education and a family centered environment but not too far from Starbucks. Tolkien wrote of a similar place that was inhabited by Hobbits who without a care in the world found refuge far north and west of human troubles in Middle Earth. Perhaps someone took excerpts from Thomas More's Utopia when devising the first cookie cutter development after World War II—a perfect society. Literary metaphors aside, the suburbs are attractive, enticing and have many good points. The outer fringes are lush and beautiful, clean, usually with good schools, new shopping malls and boutiques. Many churches that began their ministry in midtown or downtown have moved either following the congregation or leading the way, usually the former. All over the United States people from all walks of life can afford a better taste of life because in comparison to house size and standards of living in the urban jungle, the suburbs are economical and often accommodate more spacious living conditions. It's is win-win, well, not exactly.

There is an economic correlation between property and locality recognized by real estate companies and appraisers that most people are familiar with nationwide. Location is key, the property leverage and overall value of any land or building relies heavily on its location, but more importantly surroundings. The inner city of Memphis, even sections in midtown abound with aesthetic problems, as well problems in educational facilities, shopping and road problems. Though it should be noted the neighborhoods of Cooper Young and more recently Overton Square have experienced great improvement and sustainable planning. It is not only in the visual but also in the audible where Memphis does not grade well, consider noise pollution. In New York City it is part of the allure, a part of the bustling city package an all sensory treat but in Memphis this is often a deterrent for many. Suffice it to say, Memphis like many other many other cities has also a crime problem, but Memphis holds positions in the top five of every category for a city over 500,000 per capita including car theft, burglary, homicide and rape. This image is heavily supported though television, radio and especially editorials and reverberates to neighboring cities and states and stains the whole city. The media propagates this image more than any person could but it's a snapshot of a city not the city as a whole. Sadly, many of the heinous crimes are committed in a large area to the south called Orange Mound, known as the third largest ghetto in the United States. However, statistically Orange Mound is not the worst, its neighboring boroughs further east and west are worse. However, this is not Memphis, but this has become a distortion though believed as true among many Memphians white and black, rich and poor, inner and outer city. Some have stood their ground and fought back in several ways in Midtown, sections beyond Midtown to the south and downtown, and in East Memphis. Frayser now has a grand plan to revitalize, but it's a long process that needs support and traction.

Certain areas that some locals call "pockets" or enclaves have remained undisturbed and have thrived because they have remained vigilant and steadfast to any intrusions. There is opposition to any invasions that might bring down their neighborhood and threaten their safety or livelihood. Certain "filters" are put to use to maintain a safe community. One that is commonly known is economic, which eliminates many people of lower means to buy property in that area. It is simply by association that people understand those of lower means have higher possibility to commit crimes because many crimes are motivated financially. Often by this crime of financial reasons drugs are bought. Areas with drug problems cause more havoc and at the end of the day destroy families and neighborhoods. By this, keeping prices higher than market value in certain areas allows for a cushion between upper middle class and lower middle class areas and a wall of protection though not foolproof. There are cracks in the defenses and when people panic, the area falters.

One element that is peculiar and perhaps unique to Memphis is its price variance and constant changing of neighborhoods especially in Midtown. You can be on one affluent street full of 500,000 to 1 million dollar homes and proceed several blocks in any direction and totally be surrounded by government housing or a lower income sector, one that I lived in for three years. Also associated with lower income (not altogether inaccurate either) is abrasive noise, boundaries, traffic and property image. In Memphis, rock but predominantly rap intrudes the private spaces of neighbors creating tension and unknowingly to many lowering property value. Those who want to respect their neighbor recognize property boundaries physical but also visual and otherwise. Higher income housing usually includes fencing, clean separation. A German proverb states: hedges between keep friendships green. As far as traffic and property image go, the more traffic the more noise and also more vehicle clutter on the road and sadly front yards. The lawn and its maintenance is a major component of the property image, and thus its value. Poor upholding of traffic minimization (though wealthy families inherently retain more vehicles they have a more keen understanding or perhaps ability to cover them with two or four car garages) and lawn image are often the downfall of lower income families.

Another filter is to block certain developments such as government housing or worse, apartments. What a horrible thing to say, many people of all walks of life and means live in apartments.

Density, traffic and noise are the three big problems associated with apartment developments regardless of scale or class. Population density lowers values of local homes already there unless it's a condo or high-end property like downtown Memphis near the Peabody Hotel. As for clientele because a majority of those who live in apartments also use government assistance or have multiple children or have lower means—the image of apartment living is less accurate than reality. They are all nevertheless transients, nomads if you will and are subject to suspicion because many troublemakers and disturbers of the peace do not stay in one place too long. It is not only for financial profit that landlords require long contracts for renters, but it is also for stability and some familiarity. Those who wish to preserve their environs would be statistically wise to protest any developments such as these. Such is the possible fate of a newer yet established development known in Memphis as Harbortown which is beautifully secluded, with a park that country clubs with envy, from a less than becoming area across the Wolf River to its rear. Many fine houses have been built in the past twenty years since its inception but further down the main road to its north are many apartments which will invite many inhabitants over a short time—this flux of population and demographic change will usher in a devaluing of the development itself and overall decay. Harbortown has to keep a sharp eye on these trends. You may ask, where are we going with this crash course seminar on real estate protocol? The very elements of inner city strife we have observed beg the question, is it simply a matter of black and white whether a house has value or not? Does this also reflect the process by which an area has value? Also, do the demographics determine survival?

The commercial districts of areas laden with crime and surrounded by lower income housing often do not thrive, rather they die. This is the crux of urban sprawl and we can look at several relics of Memphis's commercial past to learn and try not to repeat their doom. The Raleigh Springs Mall, Mall of Memphis and what might eventually be called the late Hickory Ridge Mall have all suffered a fate or will because of demographic shift. Not completely at the fault of the area that eventually surrounds the mall, one thing each shopping center and these three malls fail to do is adapt. Southland Mall in Whitehaven a predominantly African American area is the oldest mall in Memphis and has survived and you could say done well. What separates this mall from others in Memphis? The area is middle class, educated and has been vigilant to keep the area from faltering. By extension, the mall has done well too. So is this an ethic thing or a culture thing that causes Memphis to struggle? More to come...

chapter **III**

Observations

Out of the abundance of the heart, the mouth speaks.
~ The Bible

He who jokes, confesses. – an Italian Proverb

As a man is, so he sees ~ William Blake

We swallow greedily any lie that flatters us, but we sip only little
by little at a truth we find bitter. ~Denis Diderot

Chapters 3 and 5 are collections of observations by over 1000 people over 4 years I had casual conversations with and some formal interviews. It was an even mix of black and white, lower income and white collar. Be open minded and receptive since the Freedom of Speech applies to all, and you might catch yourself agreeing with a lot of it. While I watched ABC's Prime-time: What Would You Do? I was amused how people played into one of the typical stereotyping routines when the show has an African American actor pretend he is stealing a bike. You wouldn't believe how many white people approached him and started pulling out their phones lickety-split. Would you believe in a previous scenario a white actor was not bothered and two African American ladies just walked by assuming he could have worked for the park or the fact that he is white suggested he wasn't stealing it. The same two ladies did predict the outcome correctly when they switched actor's skin color. Would you believe this was not in a southern metropolis? This new chapter discusses what white Americans generally think deep down across the US and what we can both do better. Take into account that most authors have to be careful not to crucify himself or herself and the future they wish to have in publishing books. I am making efforts to publish this first with quick succession two other books that relate with education and media in the plans that readers that are curious and introspective may want to see the other books as extensions of areas covered in various chapters of this book. One of them, education is discussed briefly, but expounded more in depth in another book I am trying to finish at this time. Nevertheless, I do hope that every reader keep in mind that I am writing with utmost sincerity and am not just sounding off but after much research echoing what people of all colors surreptitiously resonate in their E-mails, small ad-hoc conversations and the like.

Let us surmise that with grandiose generality most of us care about one another on the surface. It is tempting to imagine all is well, for most of us probably wish the world would be free of hate and anger. Before the demons come and we embrace camaraderie with our friends and discuss what is so annoying about other people—before the "mob mentality" takes hold, we do our best, and there are many people of other colors we admire, respect, even are attracted to and adore. Children believe this, it is the adults who take that away. We have all acknowledged an undercurrent of mutual distaste whether through a discussion that goes awry between two people at the doctor's office. It's all in the gaze, or tone of voice, or even slight mannerisms that resound, the verdict is out, you are a racist!

Before I traverse more dangerous waters, let me illuminate some telling actualities in the form of questions. Have you ever noticed that the lines get hazy when in situations like a movie theater or a restaurant we seem to disregard apprehension? True, we like to view movies where the crowd is respectful, though you are as likely to have an unruly raucous crowd perpetrated by white preppies than underage black teenagers—in Memphis, its sadly more often the latter. Nonetheless, there are venues where we are accepting and seem to care less about who is next to us. In a workplace, conversely, unless there is some common ground people of all colors stick with those of their same ethnicity. Have you ever noticed, we all prefer the street in which we abide to reflect our eccentricities? Though there are many streets in Memphis that form a hodgepodge of diversity, one of them I happen to live on. One trend that can be observed consistently occurring is that the number of white families moving into predominantly black areas is almost non-existent. However, large portions of white neighborhoods in Memphis have converted; gradually being replaced in droves by black families all over Memphis in the past twenty years. Why is that? Could it be that it is a matter of race relations or is it a class thing? Is it a culture thing? It is obvious, black families want a taste of the good life, It is culturally relevant and proven that urban Caucasian families are often smaller, less obtrusive and dare I say more passive. It is in modern living both in suburbia and more affluent inner city areas that the lack of noise, minimal traffic and respect for space both visual and audible those black and white families with the partiality for such things find admirable and pursue it with their paycheck.

It is confirmed by recent studies and school enrolments that those who can, being predominantly white families, send their children to private school. Memphis schools have become a sad indication of what many southern and urban American school systems have become. With many recent studies in education articulating the declining graduation rates, abysmal test scores, and rising illiteracy, few schools in the Memphis City School system maintain respectable programs (see:http://www.greatschools.org/, http://www.achievementfirst.org). They simply get by and survive the plunge with passing scores much of them not revealing the truth about the educational dilemma. I will expound on this issue later that most leaders in Memphis have the idea that throwing fresh bodies via Teach For America and federal money will fix the issue and it won't; it will be a pyrrhic victory.

So, in response to deteriorating conditions families pay for their children to attend private school most of them moving East closer to the school or move to a more economically stable and homogenous area in the suburbs and enter their children into county schools which are doing better but are starting to have some problems as well. This will all shift soon because the systems are merging. Those in largely Caucasian East Memphis either attend fairly respectable White Station or Overton High (a school for the arts) or if they can afford send their children to Memphis University School, Christian Brothers High, Evangelical Christian School, Harding Academy or St Agnes. In defense, most urban elementary schools such as Grahamwood, Idlewild and Snowden (K-8) have implemented strong core curriculum despite a system of low funding and waning teacher support system-wide. Richland Elementary is the crown jewel of the Memphis City Schools, outperforming private and Shelby County schools, but it is a rare feat. However, the middle class and lower classes suffer because the children have less accessibility to good education, though this isn't the root of the problem. Alternative schools have flourished as showcased in my Facebook page The Memphis Book and in their small number outperform most Shelby County and private schools. One could make a clear line here and say, socio-economic background does not have to be the death knell for many Memphis students, their capacity for learning is just as great if given the proper structure, not necessarily a matter of funding, but structure.

Statistically black children are far more often born of single parent families or absentee fathers. Lack of parental involvement and limiting the teachers' disciplinary latitude hinders positive growth. Schools have become huge babysitting academies and what will graduate or rather come out of these schools are perpetual generations of inept, parentless and nihilistic teenagers. This is not exclusive to black America, but is a large portion of it that will suffer greatly. Any poor area in the US will likely produce disadvantaged and uneducated youth who are prone to poverty and brushes illegal activity whether white, black or Asian or otherwise. Education by no means guarantees success, but the chances of furthering knowledge, financial growth and self-respect are exponentially larger. You perhaps might wonder however that black families, much like those of their white counterparts, rarely steer in the wrong direction when led by a core parental structure or solid figure in the family. So it is damning that in too many black families father figures are absent. It is not a matter of child identity, but it is the son who needs a father figure rather than a music video, video game or friend in the local gang.

Gang life is highly romanticized in pop and hip/hop culture (its more than just music) bent on ego-centric and divisive superfluous lyrics. It is corrosive in its nature and few teenagers or even children can differentiate the music from the product. Bill Cosby as well as his intelligent counterweight Michael Eric Dyson have sounded the knell of death for the young black community (men, in turn destroy the lives of women and the family too) if responsibility isn't taken. This wave is subtle but swift as it tarries through Memphis as an affliction. This plague is born both of black society and of its white counterparts who have made the journey difficult. One created the other, and yet the creator is somehow mad of its creation. However, much of what is holding this black generation down is self-inflicted, often relegating themselves, appearing careless and without remorse or accountability. Older generations have often been the exception who have made the journey thus far, with much tribulation and are trying to keep the ship from sinking. It seems as though they are ashamed many younger blacks as their offspring. Two steps forward, yet one step back or more. Glean from this paragraph what you wish, but there are grains of truth.

I should hope this section not be designated as ramblings of a bigot or a digression so much as a can of worms whereof I want to minimize its spillage. What has been said in this section is an assortment of what white America both in academia and in some educated circles, not excluding what some daring notable African American scholars believe. Also, where specified—we will see that which are not so much factual sentiments but myths that white America has embraced for too many years. African American culture developed a very communal group because of forced assimilation into American society both as slaves and ex-slaves during Reconstruction. This element of black culture still thrives today, much to the benefit of all but also to the detriment of their world and those surrounding them. It's a two edged sword.

It is often asked by white Americans, why did this happen, how is it that such horrible people can roam the streets raping, murdering, terrifying innocent people? One simple but crucial device that all brigands utilize is—cloak. Popular culture has given them anonymity; by this really advantageous clothing to hide both items and disguise the carrier—stylized to emulate and romanticize those on radio and in-turn music videos. Into the neighborhoods they go, and it is only apparent in white neighborhoods that something might be amiss—because everyone blends in and becomes part of the canvas in more ethnically diverse areas. Consequently it is almost impossible for honest citizens of that diverse area to differentiate the good citizen from those with bad intentions. By being given this cloak and the welcoming embrace of black culture to afford greater traffic in and out—drug dealing is just a breeze. Now, how can one ask, how does this happen? And why do innocent African Americans get shot by both white and black cops with itchy trigger fingers? Combine this clothing, fatherless children, poor education and what you have is a self-effacing world shooting themselves in the left foot just after they had the right one patched up. This not matter of debate, statistics run by the NAACP and independent groups show that education is worse for blacks, the majority of prisoners are black depending on whether it's state or local or federal prison it fluctuates from 65 to 90% in some locations—though African Americans are becoming the smaller minority behind Hispanics), and many black and white editorials (Television news, magazines and more) commenting on the demoralizing images/words depicted towards black women and grotesque materialism which is merely an illusion much the same way anorexic models fool women into thinking they have to be a size one to compete.

Let's not hide behind a guise of political correctness and sulk with righteous indignation—we must call a spade a spade and look it into the eye. Much the same way many metropolitan whites wish rednecks and militia would stay in the hills and quit embarrassing us with their obnoxious "Heritage Not Hate" bumper stickers. Many of them could tell you little of the short-lived Confederate heritage whose image has been molded into that of a beautiful pious society that was ravaged by unholy mercenaries from the North. It's not black and white, and we may never find a peaceful middle ground where Confederate Parks can be left simply as historical remnants not insensitive monuments to dark ages past for African Americans. Destroying or renaming the past is borderline revisionism—there needs to be respect on both sides, much the same way there should be nothing wrong with a statue of Malcolm X. Another element that stops progress for white and black society to coexist peacefully involves law enforcement and the bodies of government enveloping. We can look at that during the close.

To shed light on history one must open a window and let the illuminated corners and foundations of the basement (our past) be seen for what they are. Too often historical books, documentaries, novels, and media have elaborately distorted our past, both for whites and blacks. Layer by layer strata of misconception and generality have twisted the American past into two extremes. Concerning the American south between 1700 and the 1950s it has been either demonized or romanticized but the truth lies somewhere in between. What is often the reality has been something amid the two distinct parties of thought, sounds like politics doesn't it? One take, such as The Confederate States of America has a narrow small-minded interpretation of the "what if" factor had the south won the Civil War. Let me say this first, most whites today in the south are happy that the north had won, however, it was called the war of northern aggression for a reason. Most historians whose focus is the 19th century state clearly that slavery would have most likely phased out before 1880 or 1900 at the latest. The shift of the factory based north, ban on the slave trade across the Atlantic after Britain pulled the trigger and a growing US that many even in the south didn't support slavery because only 2% of the American populous owned slaves, north and south. This is not to excuse slavery, but to illuminate that just facts will lend truth to certain myths about our past.

It is true one cannot discuss the past without filtering the minutiae with bias. Nevertheless, there are those of us on both sides of the ethnic line who choose a transparent portrayal of history over agenda driven propaganda. Let us divulge the past cautiously together. Racism is rooted both in truth and lies. Deception often is unchecked by those who wrote history. One dominating rule is that the victor records the battle—so an extension of that would be the ruler held authority over what got published. Without hidden records or diaries we might not have known much of the details around the Holocaust. Similarly, we might not have understood slavery both in its humane and cruel nature. In the Americas was it not for some educated slaves, abolitionists and records of the owners themselves the details of slavery would be like mythology, partly true partly conjecture. Though in small number, one hundred years before the American Civil War many settlers were black and acquiring land and owning African slaves themselves. This is something not even mentioned as a side note in academia or pop culture history (movies, songs etc.). Only a small percentage of southerners owned slaves, but it is true many who owned slaves adopted the Willie Lynch doctrine of disciplining and "caring" of slaves (to be covered in the next chapter) . So, we need to delve in the history of slavery.

chapter IV

A little history

If you want to understand today, you have to search yesterday.
~Pearl Buck

People are trapped in history, and history is trapped in them.
~James Baldwin, Notes of a Native Son

Professor Johnston often said that if you didn't know history, you
didn't know anything. You were a leaf that didn't know it was part
of a tree. ~Michael Crichton, Timeline

History is filled with the sound of silken slippers going downstairs
and wooden shoes coming up. ~Voltaire

History teaches us the mistakes we are going to make. ~Author
Unknown

This is crucial that we understand the roots of African American culture and how it was shaped over time. Not that we will be privy to all elements of African American culture, but that we can appreciate their struggle and ultimately their culture. Slavery being nothing new to civilization on every continent (except Australia) was at its height during Imperial Roman rule (1st century AD-4th century AD). It was exhibited in forms of house servant all the way down to degrading tasks such as 16-hour days in the mines of Anatolia (modern day Turkey). Between Roman rule and the Renaissance (500 and 1500 AD) slavery in Europe evolved primarily into serfdom while in Africa and Asia it was even more benign for one-thousand years when Islamic Kingdoms held sway over most of the known world, even in Spain. There were parallels of slavery in India and China and further east but these civilizations had little impact on modern America. As Basil Davidson writes in The African Slave Trade, the slaves "status, often, was comparable to that of the men and woman in Western Europe throughout medieval times. In this respect Africa and Europe, at the beginning of their connection, traded and met as equals." The discovery of the New World brought new wealth to Europe and for everyone involved in what was designated the "The Triangular Trade." Kevin Shillington writes, "the colonizers soon felt the need for a large imported labour force to work the gold and silver mines of the mainland and their tobacco plantations on the islands."

Starting in the 16th century and going as late as the 1890s slaves were abstracted from emerging states such as Benin, Oyo, Denkyira and Akwamu that were kingdoms between Angola and Senegal (Western Sub-Saharan Africa). From this coast Europeans (primarily Spanish, Dutch, French, Dane, and English—the latter prohibited slavery in the early 19th century) traded goods for captured Africans worth exponentially more than a lifework as a freeman. From there the "property" or "cargo" in the words of contemporaries was extradited on a treacherous voyage named today the "Atlantic Slave Trade." The end was sometimes in the West Indies or South America, and then some were brought further into the plantation states. Plantation crops were shipped to Europe, wherein manufactured goods were sent to Africa for trade of slaves or simply sold. All three continents benefited on the surface, but African states were gradually becoming pawns and having to sell larger numbers to support demand. This was a slow embezzlement of the people and stability of western African (it was only to get worse under European Imperialism at the turn of the 20th century). This trend continued and affected the same areas until there were only remnants of civilizations; an estimated 10 million slaves were taken to the new world, while another two million perished on the trans-Atlantic voyage. One may ask, why Native Americans weren't used to work the land and mine? Simply put, Africans were gathered in larger numbers (settlements or towns), already skilled for the job, built physically better for tropical and southern climates, had great immunity to European diseases like smallpox and measles (which killed more Native Americans than war ever could) and did not wreak havoc on settlements like the Iroquois and Chickasaw nations had already done for early Spanish and British explorers.

Ultimately color became the clear separating trait whereby simply being a Negro was presumptive of a slave status in North American states. Manumission, a process honored for centuries in the old world whereby one could earn their freedom was becoming difficult and in the mid-19th century laws in Georgia and Mississippi were discriminatory towards owners to grant freedom to slaves. Slavery was becoming more malignant, even after the journey across the Atlantic after several uprisings the tactics started to change. A man named Willie Lynch introduced a methodology that today still resonates in the culture fabric of our nation and is clearly evident. Rather than go further I think quoting what is called the Willie Lynch Letter first will shed light on historical matters in the US:

I greet you here on the bank of the James River in the year of our Lord, one thousand seven hundred and twelve. First I shall thank you, the Gentlemen of the Colony of Virginia, for bringing me here. I am here to help you solve some of your problems with slaves. Your invitation reached me on my modest plantation in the West Indies where I have experimented with some of the newest and still the oldest methods for control of slaves. Ancient Rome would envy us if my program is implemented. As our boat sailed south on the James River, named for our illustrious King James, whose bible we cherish, I saw enough to know that your program is not unique. While Rome used cords of wood as crosses for standing human bodies along the old highways in great numbers, you are here using the tree and the rope on occasion.

I caught the whiff of a dead slave hanging from a tree a couple of miles back. You are not only losing valuable stock by hangings, you are having uprisings, slaves are running away, your crops are sometimes left in the fields too long for maximum profit, you suffer occasional fires, your animals are killed, gentlemen...you know what your problems are; I do not need to elaborate. I am not here to enumerate your problems, I am here to introduce you to a method of solving them.

In my bag here, I have a fool-proof method for controlling your black slaves. I guarantee everyone of you that if installed correctly it will control the slaves for at least 300 years. My method is simple, any member of your family or any overseer can use it.

I have outlined a number of differences among the slaves, and I take these differences and make them bigger. I use fear, distrust, and envy for control purposes. These methods have worked on my modest plantation in the West Indies, and it will work throughout the South. Take this simple little test of differences and think about them. On the top of my list is "Age", but it is there because it only starts with an "A"; the second is "Color" or shade; there is intelligence, size, sex, size of plantations, attitude of owners, whether the slaves live in the valley, on a hill, East, West, North, South, have fine or coarse hair, or is tall or short. Now that you have a list of differences, I shall give you an outline of action—but before that, I shall assure you that distrust is stronger than trust, and envy is stronger than adulation, respect, or admiration.

The Black Slave, after receiving this indoctrination, shall carry on and will become self-refueling and self-generating for hundreds of years, maybe thousands.

Don't forget, you must pitch the old Black vs. the young Black male, and the young Black male against the old Black male. You must use the dark skinned slaves vs the light skinned slaves, and the light skinned slaves vs. the dark skinned slaves. You must use the female vs. the male, and the male vs. the female. You must also have your servants and overseers distrust all Blacks, but it is necessary that your slaves trust and depend on us. They must love, respect, and trust only us.

Gentlemen, these kits are your keys to control, use them. Have your wives and children use them. Never miss opportunity. My plan is guaranteed, and the good thing about this plan is that if used intensely for one year, the slaves themselves will remain perpetually distrustful.

This document speaks for itself and illuminates what may be for many the underlying divisions in the black community still today. We will come back to these matters, but let us first finish the essential historical overview. In the early 1800s industrialism shook the western world bringing many of those in rural areas (the largest influx into cities until World War II) into urban settings modernizing in many ways the livelihood but also the necessities of a workforce and the mindset. It seemed that with this infrastructural shift slavery was declining in necessity and became a luxury for affluent families both old and new in the North. Scholars and everyone else have confused this as a leaning towards tolerance and equality in the North. Conversely, slavery was still needed in the south to manage large tracts of property still producing exponentially more cotton, tobacco and other crops. While in the north blacks were relegated from freeman to proletariat (working class low wage factory worker) or slave to workman, some were educated along the way with help from white supporters. More responsibility (financial-food-etc.) and stress was placed on the independence of blacks in society—for some this was opportunity for most it impoverished them (for which there were small numbers in the north mind you).

Long had northern states relied on the South's wealth for leverage—if it had not been for the southern states it is possible both the victory over Britain in the War of Independence and the War of 1812, and also Mexico thirty years later would have been nearly impossible—the United States would most likely have not developed so quickly from the 1820s onward. Without the raw materials, the north would have had greater troubles bartering and forming wealthy trade agreements with Europe and elsewhere. The south was not an annoying stepchild that many historians and media portray today and in Americas past—it was a remnant of a world lost to science and industry, a land of chivalry, as well as a land of power, wealth and history. This is not to say, the south was sensitive to changing world views about slavery, but their religious beliefs were assimilated into African culture and to this day sing and worship many in the same fashion in remembrance and gladness.

That was a quick study that could require complementary reading for some, but in essence, the past make us who we are and would explain a lot that seems to confuse people today who don't know history. The equation is simply this: African Americans were forged by their captors and by abolitionists who pushed for their freedom, but have yet to be received as the abolitionists intended. The years after the Civil War in the north and south slaves did not venture far from their plantations or dwellings. As industrialism grew some migrated to large cities like Chicago and Detroit and Los Angeles, but a large majority who still reside in the Southeast did not leave and the once cordial pre Civil War relationship between whites and blacks faded and developed into a great rift spawned by indifference, stereotypes, northern interference and southern stupidity. Yes, documents and sources show that as a whole, relations in public spaces before the tensions rose in the 1860s over slavery that blacks owned slaves, held positions in office, and had amiable relations with whites. It was a crock pot recipe that made the south what it is today, and the circles vary from Aryan Nation hatred to just simple apathy and genuine love from whites towards blacks. The complex ideology and ecosystem of racism that subsists today was created by generations of white Americans centuries back but the fire is enraged by the last thirty years of black culture that some of whom want to piss on the efforts of their predecessors. I use the word some, because I am close friends with many loving, and positive African Americans who are like minded and don't appreciate the counterproductive efforts of people in their own ethnic group, many of which propagate myths and are a detriment to the prosperity of African Americans everywhere. I will elaborate in this next chapter.

chapter V

What proliferates the negative images towards African Americans?

I wish Google maps had an, 'Avoid The Ghetto Route' option.
~ unknown

I don't think of myself as a poor deprived ghetto girl who made good. I think of myself as somebody who from an early age knew I was responsible for myself, and I had to make good. ~ Oprah Winfrey

First, pretend this is a letter from mainstream white America and a majority of black America pleading to the minority group of black Americans who have not bought into this book yet and may never. One must try. One of the images that stand out that is derogatory to black culture is the video of Nelly sliding his credit card through the butt crack of a voluptuous African American woman. It is in burned into the minds of many who saw it and became a rallying image for those such as Bill Cosby and Michael Eric Dyson to proselytize the gospel of change for African Americans in the late 90s and early 2000s. What is disconcerting is that much the same way many whites embrace the 70s and 80s and relive those decades in band tours, blacks relive their youth through music of the past—and yet, the youth of white America today many of them have a mix mash of contemporary pop and alternative, and some music of the past.

Why is that with exception to cultured (raised with an appreciation for a variety of music, the arts etc.) blacks are they so doggedly provincial? Or is that the image and not the truth? Caught in their world of music and movies that are persistently demeaning to themselves, minorities, women, and only tear down the world they inhabit seem perpetually damning. This practice is as if to piss on their existence and then complain about it. Gangsta rap is not without some clever nuance and poetry, but only by some exceptions. When a whole generation of youth and young workers play this music which is not only loud enough in bass as to violate noise pollution laws but repetitive synthetically produced drivel and unoriginal at best. The imagery it draws upon has little redeeming value. Often artists try to justify their craft as accurate depictions the life in the hood, telling a story, keeping it real and other countless clichés of depravity. True there are horrible conditions, but rap is rarely a documentary and usually a sensational appraisal of the life they once lived or still do, it is not trying to escape but relish. This is how most of the youth see it, go ask them. To delight in and make money in the process while lead countless others in black America and some even in white America to believe that all cops are bad, don't trust the white man, make money by all means, drug usage is cool and the list goes on. So, when rap artists come on and try to wax eloquently about how they want to get the word out on how the life in gangs is wrong and people need to pay attention to the needs of urban youth, it would be more believable if they would stop getting arrested for drug possession or spousal abuse. It's the blind leading the blind, and sadly, some African Americans go to church and when they get home, turn on the same crap—tell me who to take seriously here? Remember, this is a collection of thoughts coming from numerous interviews, white and black Mid-Southerners, so you digest it and take the journey to the finish.

There is more to say, but you surely see where I was going. Clothing, lets approach this from the most rational point possible. Form verses function, are baggy clothes that drag to the ground simply useful? You would have to say no, except that it is much easier to conceal weapons and drugs when you have multiple pockets and spacious clothing. Clothes dragging below the waist are offensive to most people, yet African Americans (and some "wannabe" whites) are Hell-bent on continuing this style, though its not practical and most women who are ok with it have problems of keeping their legs crossed—that's one reason it goes on, it works for them and most cities are not establishing public decency laws or enforcing them. So, with men who want to be taken seriously, yet continue to walk around, drag their pants, practically pay an homage to gansta life seem to be upset when they are targeted by cops and security—see how absurd this style really is. Most African Americans past the age of 40 have no compassion for this lewd fashion and lifestyle if you want to call it such. Women wearing more revealing clothes with bodies that need to be covered more modestly don't receive unwanted attention as much but often demean themselves and then get upset when they don't get respect. If it quacks like a duck and walks like one, then it's a whore, isn't that usually the case. The perception of self-respect has to be solidified before you receive respect, both for the male and female. If you want to represent your culture, your families, your heritage best, then show that you can rise above this mockery of culture that is self-destructive and fruitless. Great you made an album, now you are the jester of the month, see how your legacy will fizzle and your children and your following will go on without direction and repeat the same errors.

The treatment of African American women, or the plight— Dyson writes several illuminating stories on the self-destructive nature of courtship and the social scene for young and ambitious black women. Sure, those who depict themselves in a less than flattering light (lack of clothing, poor speech etc.) get what's coming to them, but what about those with achievement after achievement, what about them? I have several black female friends with the same wrap, and have come to different conclusions, one of which may just be to broaden the net, don't lower your standards but be realistic. Movies have been made with this central theme. The way some are treated is because they don't treat themselves with respect. In other cases men have been indoctrinated with a strange affection for matriarchal authority but not for the woman they want to bed, a 180 degree ideological change from yes ma'am to shut up and bend over. This stems often from that video (and countless like them) and songs I mentioned in the opening of this chapter. When you have constant bombardment of Mp3 players in the ear, you start to absorb the information into your own modus operandi or as once said, reality complex. It starts to govern your decision making and so garbage in garbage out. You hear and see how women are treated, you start having reflex decision based on how you see women treated.

Speech: do I need to write a paragraph about this, perhaps. Many who read this may find it like nails on the chalkboard. Let us quickly venture into this well-known phenomenon known as Ebonics by some and by other names that are currently being invented. It's not a matter of accents, my wife has one of those and so do my cousins in Mississippi. It's not a matter of verbiage like a great rapper Common or NAS would use but the incorrect pronunciation and grammatical violations that take place on live TV that embarrass me as a Memphian and with certainty embarrass countless African

Americans who know how to articulate with poise and conviction. I get embarrassed when I am witness to a white man on television or in some editorial spouting out some language that would make Shakespeare heave usually complaining about an issue over their mutt dog or a scuffle at Wal-Mart. What is striking about Ebonics is the shameless ignorance it displays as well as the self-effacing witlessness. Words turn on themselves and slang that change at a moment's notice because someone hit wonder rapper with an electronically modified chant institutes new vernacular. It is a disparaging sub language that originates in low income areas white and black and is distributed through media, school and everywhere in between including Facebook and Twitter. Little do many who use it known that it changes their writing and communication skills limiting upward movement in most fields. Hedging your bets on making it in the NBA where speaking skills are lacking or in music where rhyme doesn't have to rhyme anymore and nor do words have to previously exist is a deprived reality. Too many students are pressed enough with this message that plan A probably won't happen (I am covering this in another book quite thoroughly) and the way you talk and seem to write won't cut it either. Tinted windows and extravagant revamped cars are not an outlandish concept here in Memphis but a common item in the cityscape. Often men of youth and men well into their 40s drive slowly by to advertise their work, occasionally stopping for the ladies or making a deal, you can't tell sometimes. Blending in part with illegal activity they eulogize rap artists and people of ill repute through material. This is a lifestyle to them that to the outside world resembles crime. Funny enough, many of these same law abiding citizens get upset when targeted by cops. Shouldn't they be singled out? What do criminals usually like to use for disguise, tinted windows, and what do most drug dealers and pimps have as their ride of choice a 70s or 80s or early 90s souped up car with plenty of space. These citizens propagate the myth that a thug life is cool, the image they portray is misleading to youth, cops, whites, and even more importantly older African Americans who would rather drive a car that resembles factory specks and appear legitimate. This leads me to the over theme in this chapter—a self-destructive cycle produced by those destroying themselves. For centuries the baton of oppression and hatred was held by whites and has been passed to culture (not a majority but a large enough number) of African Americans where they are now inflicting it upon themselves.

The inherent problems in rap, urban clothing, treatment of women in media, Ebonics and with the obsession with cars and tinted windows are all interrelated and collectively create the farce that is the African American obsession with material gain which surpasses those of middle class whites. They extol the very things that are corrosive, indecent and unproductive in the end. Ask most rap artists that "made it," often they will tell you that dealing drugs is wrong and that gang violence is wrong, they made a lot of money off of it, but with a tone of irresponsibility and smugness they contend that getting into film or television saved them, not rap. If countless juveniles are hoping that odds will shift their way and they will get a label to sign them or they will rise up in the ranks of a cartel they often find themselves six feet under, in prison or worse—back in the hood with children they don't know exist strung up on meth. Clothing that is demeaning unto itself which makes the woman wearing it no better than a piece of meat should come with some kind of warning label: clothing severely lowers your worth, men will objectify you, and if raped, we are not liable, you have been warned. This is not to say rape is justified, but it is to suggest that the carrots dangling in front of the turtle can be misleading. Media plays toys with this image of demeaning women, some female artists try to make it sexy only to be slapped around by their boyfriend off set. Speech that is neither edifying or intelligible much like more gangster rap is humorous to many Europeans with a higher GDP who dance to it in nocturnal clubs for escape but go back to their condos in Berlin, Paris, Amsterdam or London and sleep a good sleep knowing they won't be shot, have two months paid vacation, travel the globe and live twenty years longer.

The tinted windows and wheels on crack add fuel to the fire because it's the most public image blacks portray to society besides media and often it's the most damaging because it makes a mockery on itself. There is a saying amongst middle class that poor people have nice cars and crappy houses because they want to portray success while wealthy will drive in anything European old or new because they know they have a mansion back home and don't have a hang-up about their image. This has some truth to it. Psychologist will tell you those who try the hardest to look wealthy in public have an inferiority complex, as you will see in historical academia where professors strain to link Egypt's glorious Empires to sub-Saharan Africa (that's another book). I stepped on some toes perhaps when I stated that the African American obsession material gain surpasses those of middle class whites, but you know that some church members and others are ripe with people who over-indulge in self appraising pretentiousness. Whites fill churches just as well as blacks looking for health and wealth gospel message like a certain pastor in Houston, but the efforts made to look wealthy by blacks far outweigh those of whites in the world of media. It has a damaging effect to the psyche of young individuals who believe material gain brings happiness, but usually brings taxes, divorces and a downsizing often below the original beginnings of the artists. To take the viewer on that fantasy that you too can succeed and live the high life is what some light hearted Hip Hop video seem to portray, but in most cases as with rap the obsession with cash, gold, cars and cribs (houses) sets the tone for children to lose their vision in school of getting an education. Many students lose their way because media (not to be confused with all media generally music videos and music) tells them that education didn't bring them fame, living the pimp life, shooting and doing drugs got them there. Such is the fate of many African American youth and young adults because the older generation who spawned them have given up in many cases, washed their hands of it or struggle to assist their grandchildren with their homework.

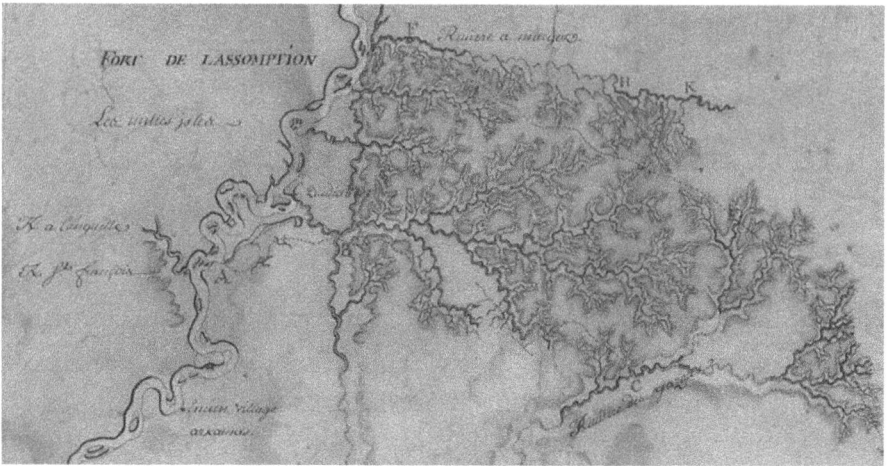

The location (18th century) of where Memphis would eventually be established along the 3rd Chickasaw bluff. The area was first settled by the Mississippian Culture and then by the Chickasaw Native Americans. For millennia they occupied the bluffs along the Mississippi River building a large mound on the bluff. European exploration came later, beginning in the 16th century with Spanish explorer Hernando de Soto (whom we named a bridge after) and French explorers led by Cavelier and La Salle.

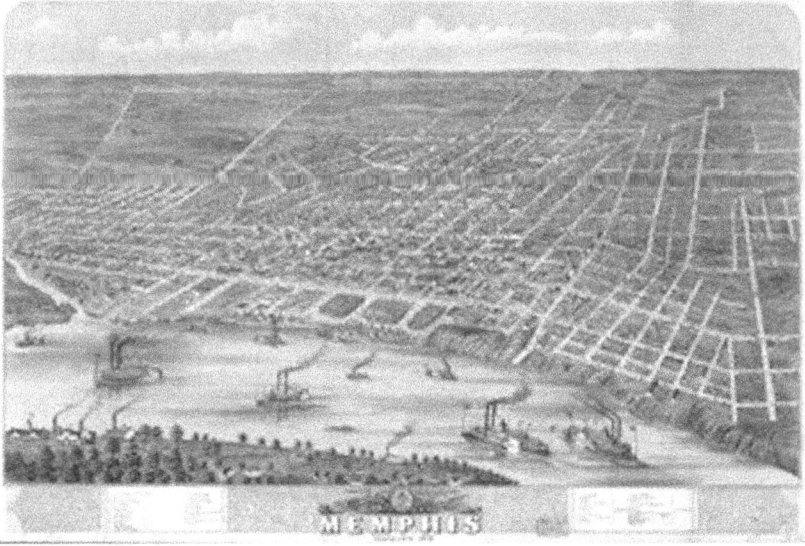

Just like Alexander, London, Boston or Hong Kong a growing city historically has always benefitted from a strong port or access to water where trade can flourish. This created a backdrop where Memphis and the delta region would be blessed and cursed with a memory of slavery. The beneficiary of this memory is the art of blues, rock and roll and a cross section of American music for decades. One could argue Memphis is the greatest epicenter of artists, musicians, actors, actresses and singers the United States has ever had and it is on full display every weekend on Beale Street and other venues on South Main, in Cooper Young, in Overton Square and others.

Between 1880 and 1920, Memphis experienced growth nearly unparalleled by any other city in the US including New York City, Chicago, Los Angeles. In fact, you might confuse downtown Memphis with one of them in that day. There is a disconnect between what historians will tell you about our glorious past and what 95% of Memphians and newcomers will think if you were to ask them. What is not told is that much of the change for good and bad has been at the hands of local leaders who were in their capacity and vision made choices that either elevated or in most cases set Memphis back behind the growing metropolitan cities of the mid-20th century. Translation, the culprit was not the Yellow Fever for that was long gone when Memphis started to show life and vibrancy again. There were some good decisions in our city's past made like protesting a route of I-40 through Midtown in 1957 that lasted until the 1970s, but those same sentiments are misguided today that stop green friendly bluff development. Our city is that of enterprise and entrepreneurial ingenuity with companies like Greyhound, Piggly Wiggly, Holiday Inn and Pinnacle all founded here but made their Exodus or demise due to mismanagement. We waste what good we have and squander chances of getting more by allowing poor leadership at the helm. The most disturbing narrative in our tale is the apathy or perhaps oblivious mindsets of historians and politicians alike that we are anywhere close to what we could have been, but this book will show how far we fell and how far we need to go to be what we should have been.

Horse racing rivaled the Kentucky Derby for decades and some historians would argue horse racing in Memphis was second to none, until in 1905 it was banned. Unlike most reports, it was not Memphis locals but the legislature in Nashville that was the reason it was banned and thus crippling the economic growth of a promising city. This is one instance among many where the foundational aspects of Memphis were superior to many cities all over the US, but the negligence of leaders and politicians led us astray after World War I and have only shown glimpses of hope and vision since. The last five years feels promising, but it pales in comparison of our national prestige we commanded in the early 1900s.

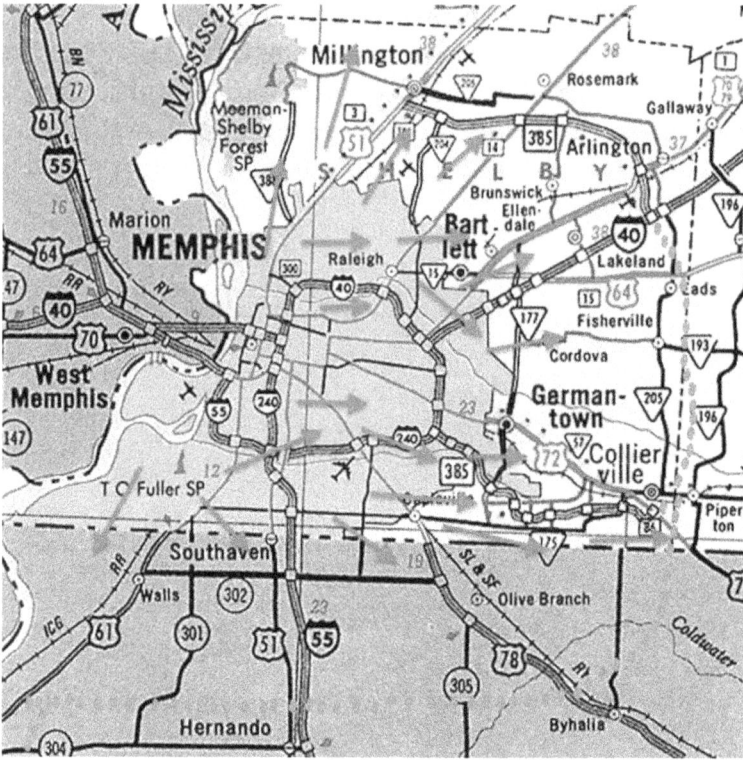

To people not familiar this would appear like wind patterns of a meteorological kind but this is actually the pattern of blight/white flight from 1960s Memphis until present day. One is the lion and the other the gazelle, read the book to discover the motivations and intricacies of this problem that still presses the middle class further out and creates poverty stricken, commercially dead and crime filled chasms. Poor education is in the midst of this battle and we will address that issue an several others in due time. My book coming March 2013 entitled *The Education Artifice* fleshes out the conundrum of public education highlighting the school systems of this area.

This is a recent crime map (2012) where the dark hues represent areas that are low in crime while the lighter shades indicate areas high in crime. This is from collected data encompassing burglaries, rapes, homicides, assaults and all other forms imaginable that could be labeled as crime. Notice the link between Midtown and Germantown via the Walnut Grove/Poplar corridor. Midtown has the distinction of being the most diverse section (socially-economically, ethnically etc) of the Memphis metropolitan area, the crossroads of many commercial districts, and having the dubious distinction of being dangerous to people all over Memphis and in the suburbs (including the outlying towns). If we cannot overcome such a myth about midtown which is also experiencing the greatest development (Overton Square, The Kroc Center, Sears Crosstown, Broad Arts District and more) and notoriety world-wide then Memphis will not get out of its own way. Downtown receives a similar wrap which is equally false.

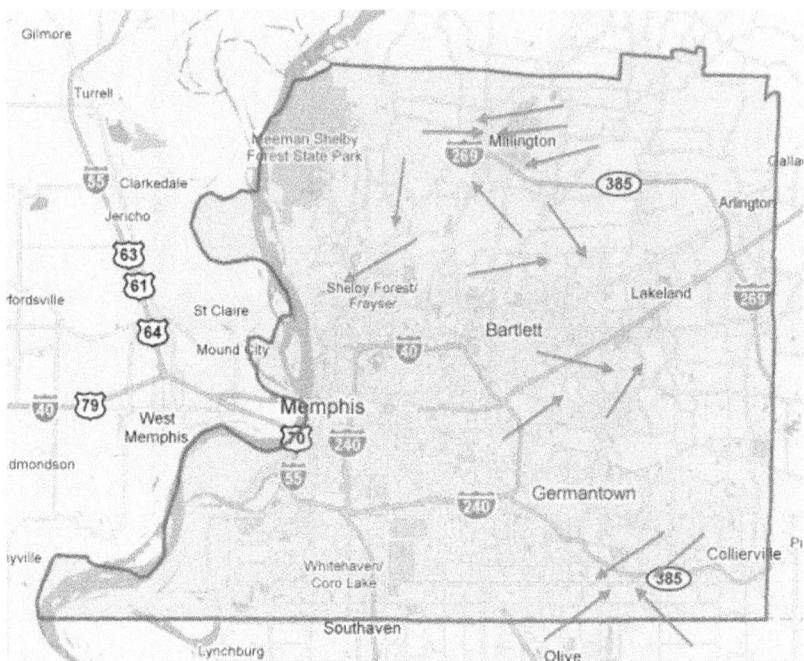

This map shows low performing Shelby County Schools that rank almost parallel with the lowest performing Memphis City Schools, however this is not realized by people living in the suburbs. There is a myth which has been a major catalyst for the municipal school movements from Millington to Bartlett to Lakeland and Arlington and down to Germantown and Collierville that the Shelby County Schools (SCS) are light years ahead of Memphis City Schools (MCS). Well, this is only partly true. The elementary schools of MCS have poor test scores and reviews in certain areas of Memphis as well as SCS in certain areas of Shelby County. The structure that envelopes the curriculum, teacher recruiting and other aspects of both school systems is not that much different between the two systems. However, the HR and overall administration at MCS is not a well oil machine while SCS is fairly well run. The real problems in both Shelby County and City School which are merging are in the middle schools where parent's participation drops, children experience the most drastic physical and emotional changes and the opposite sexes discover one another. Furthermore by this time children have discovered that their grades do not count until High School and that punishment is inconsistent at best. Only a few schools in Shelby County have a proper system in place to handle this rapid transition from elementary child to middle school youth. MCS is likened to the Titanic, too big, slow to change course, and dysfunctional in turbulence (which is the case in many MCSchools). A Shelby County School can only be deemed better where the neighborhood around it reflects a stable socio-economic background, strong family values and less bussing. This is a fading percentage on the fringes where with city ends and the towns begin. Hence, it is a more complex matter than just SCS v MCS, it's really about people that are like minded circling the wagons amongst other things that are discussed in the book.

The arrows indicate the top tourist attractions from Tripadvisor.com 2012. The concentration is of course midtown and downtown only with the exception of Graceland (the home of Elvis Presley) in Whitehaven, however the majority of hotels are outside the loop with only a fraction downtown. There are smaller cities in the American South that have more hotel rooms than Memphis, this creates a problem drawing conferences and large venues to downtown. Building hotels away from tourism is counterintuitive and presses the idea of further interstate development outside of the city limits thus pushing hotels and commerce to those major transportation routes. In Memphis, when an area (neighborhood association and interested parties) allows development usually to their east it creates a migration of commerce often to the detriment of the neighborhood too unaware of what is about to transpire. See the next image.

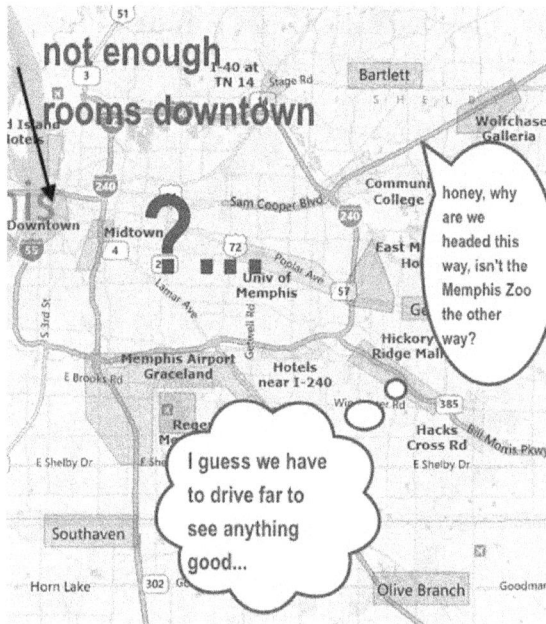

The need for hotel rooms in a city that has many growing tourist attractions primarily in midtown and downtown is paramount. Too often this is left to the mercy of private groups wanting to invest locally where instead we should be offering incentives that are legislatively and economically advantageous to the investor. Much the same way our city is ripe with distinctive and unique locations that would make filming a delight to many directors and producers, the legislature based in Nashville and our local representatives are inept to stir change in policies (tax incentives, friendly contracting with local sound and lighting companies) that would attract more filmmaking in a city that cries out for moviemaking. Hotels, tourism and filmmaking are interrelated in many ways, the most important element is the packaging that Memphis is a delectable, diverse and welcoming place and we want you to stay in the midst of it, not on the outskirts.

In our ongoing Renaissance we must endeavor to produce self-sustaining venues that do not rely perpetually on the generosity of private funds or taxes. Tourism, filmmaking, and the hotel industry all would enhance this funding. Also, we must link these commercial districts and attractions with the rest of Memphis via modern transportation. The book paints a picture quite clear that we are segmented much to the thanks of Memphians not traveling outside their comfort zone but also to the poor transportation system (i.e. antiquated interstate, MATA, and more). With the exception of the grid system of Midtown and green spaces with bike trails linking them, we are a discombobulated experience for residents who Facebook their grievances and visitors who often do not repeat their visit.

Here is a diagram correlating the two key elements of my book: commerce and education which if working properly will suppress the socio-economic segmentation and crime that keeps our city from moving forward and being globally competitive.

The circle is an approximate boundary of Midtown. Keep in mind, Midtown is the quintessential heart of a city where its identity, tourism and very soul thrive. Downtown is the brother in many ways. There are several other sections of Memphis where what I describe will also apply, but not all simultaneously.

The arrows pointing outward signify the migration of Midtown residents to the outlying areas usually the suburbs. The migration is thought to be motivated by white/blight flight, but in Midtown's case, it is primarily the lack of quality public education. Notice the arrow to the airport will signify leaving Memphis entirely for which this comprises almost a third of Midtown residents by some recent estimates.

The arrows pointing inward signify the residents that will descend upon Midtown every day from everywhere even the Mid-South and make their home in Midtown for a period of their life. The attraction of Midtown is the cosmopolitan dynamic where jobs, night life, history, the proximity to downtown and other great areas east and other intangibles that people from other areas of the US and World love about Midtown Memphis

Midtown has experienced such a Renaissance in commerce, development, green friendly initiatives and modernization including improved museums and attractions, what it needs more of is quality public schools along the caliber of Richland and Grahamwood further east. There are a few respectable public schools in midtown but not enough to cater to the demands. Parents line up outside once a year at the Board of Education for days camping overnight to get a number hoping to land one of these schools for their child or children. A house three blocks from a highly respectable Rhodes College and in a historical district is zoned for a poorly reviewed elementary school and even worse middle school. The once great schools of midtown have slipped since the 80s. Midtown is unpredictable and always evolving (something not considered by business planners) because the working class/middle class base grows up from their 20s to 30s and meanwhile have kids and are faced to move where they can afford good public schools or fork out a lot of money for private. It creates a state of socio-economic flux from the interior outward that political scientists, economist and statisticians have not caught because they are looking at only a small sampling of the canvas. It is a problem Memphis has to face before commerce can be stable, crime decline, our transportation infrastructure can grow (Airport included) and a segmented Memphis can unify literary and figuratively to the extent that the people of Memphis have confidence in our city once again.

chapter VI

Hey, what happened to the malls?

A racially integrated community is a chronological term timed from the entrance of the first black family to the exit of the last white family. ~Saul Alinsky

All cities are mad: but the madness is gallant. All cities are beautiful: but the beauty is grim. ~Christopher Morley, Where the Blue Begins

I have an affection for a great city. I feel safe in the neighbourhood of man, and enjoy the sweet security of the streets. ~Henry Wadsworth Longfellow

As I type this segment of the book, at least for today I endeavor to focus and not be distracted by the sounds of phone going off in the main public library just between Walnut Grove and Poplar in the eastern section of Midtown. You might wonder what is the point in mentioning the location? Well, like some cities with great diversity they have crossroads or intersections where you can clearly see the change in demographics just outside your window. Literally outside the windows from the fourth floor an affluent area just across the street to the south with houses valued over 500,000 (by the way, that's like 2,000,000+ in New York City terms) decorates the landscape, while the modern library dominates the area between Poplar and Walnut Grove. To the north is an area most notably in the headlines for the massacre of five people by one man, notorious for its crime, army barrack style government housing and a fairly new Police Precinct. A few good throws from Peyton Manning and you could reach Tillman from Chickasaw Gardens. I gather information on an area much like this one several miles to the West called Cooper Young.

A committee was put together concerning the redevelopment of the Mid-south fairgrounds. It was a through verbose study of the economic, demographic and cultural history of the mid-south fairgrounds located off East Parkway bordered of the other sides by what is now called Orange Mound, Buntyn and Christian Brothers University. What struck me, as in the past, is how great Memphis once was. Most people uninformed of their own past often neglect to observe past of the city in which they have matured. It was as it is with most historians a very seductive experience to look at old photos, look back upon more innocent times, reminisce, and wax nostalgic. Nevertheless it is very telling when you look at 1920s Memphis and it has the strange similarity to 1920s New York City, you wonder, what went wrong? True every city has this inherent pendulum of prosperity and destitution whereby most major cities undulate. However, most cities have never seem the rise and fall of such a city as this one, and what is scary most of all is that most Memphians don't see the underlying dangers. The obvious signs manifest themselves in waffling politicians, mothballed and dilapidated buildings that litter the cityscape and record breaking numbers in homicides, car break-ins, burglaries and the list goes on placing Memphis in the top 5 in the US with these categories. However, the writing on the wall shows itself in other forms but people dismiss it as normal reactions to urban sprawl, simply changing areas. Here is where the rubber meets the road.

It's entirely possible that Longfellow could have enjoyed Memphis when he spoke of "sweet security of the streets" depending on the area of which he spoke and what decade. You may want to ask, what does shopping have to do with ethnic turmoil or prosperity, well, if you can see that the economic backbone of many cities is shopping and tourism and that the moral and social dilapidation of our fair city will lead to its downfall if the core of the city keeps rotting from within, pushing the money (affluent citizens) further out so far that they cannot benefit the city, contribute (shop, buy tickets) be taxed or care to give back—a damaging disconnect.. Most cities cannot compare though you could argue that there are similarities in urban metros across the south, northeast and certain cities west of the Mississippi. The commercial enterprises of areas laden with crime and surrounded by lower income housing often do not thrive, rather they die. This is the crux of urban sprawl and we can look at several relics of Memphis's commercial past to learn and try not to repeat their doom. The Raleigh Springs Mall, Mall of Memphis and what may soon be called the late Hickory Ridge Mall have all suffered a fate or will because of demographic shift. Not completely at the fault of the area that eventually surrounds the mall, one thing each shopping center and these three malls fail to do is adapt. What does this have to do with color or race or ethnicity—in one word, everything.

Let's go back four decades during the height of the civil rights movement. Some can still remember the unwelcome eyes, the signs that said, whites only or black restroom. The dilapidated schools, buildings with insufficient facilities, poor materials and unequal access to educational materials that most whites had at their fingertips were a glaring injustice. The black people only signs and Jim Crow laws were salt on the wounds of blacks who served their country, made honest living, and were only a few generations from slavery. Many adult African Americans of the time were divided into two camps, the King-way or the X-way, some waffled in between. Though Malcolm X later changed his views of violent protest after a visit to Mecca, the seeds of aggressive tactics had formed, not only in the Nation of Islam but in the Black Panthers, Detroit and LA gangs that would grow in the 70s. The shift took place in this time from a passive African American general to splinter groups, though a small minority, would influence inner city youth and corrode the minds and spirits of generations ahead.

Let us go forward, in the 1970s Memphis had already overcome change, the King assassination, riots, recessions, and political upheaval. Midtown took change with a grain of salt and stayed the course. Whitehaven, whose name was going to be oxymoronic in time did change well or didn't depending on the color of the person telling this story, mostly a change in demographics, the same can be said concerning Frayser. As factories in the area began to close, the population of Frayser began to markedly dwindle in the 1970s and 80s, and it stands at 51,068 today. With a large majority of its residents earning incomes below the poverty line, only 6% holding college degrees, and a continued lack of business and industrial investment, the neighborhood is now one of the most economically depressed & highest crime-rated areas of Memphis. Whitehaven experienced an almost mirror image, originally a farm community, Whitehaven was developed as a white residential suburb of Memphis in the 1950s and early 1960s. In 1950 Whitehaven had a population of 1,311. In 1960 Whitehaven had a population of 13,894 Whitehaven was annexed by the city of Memphis January 1, 1970. Whitehaven was integrated in the late 1960s and white flight ensued over the next two decades. The stark difference is that in Whitehaven the annexation of Memphis sparked the demographic shift while in Frayser's the loss of companies like Firestone brought on financial loss to the community which to this day is like a ghost town without any central shopping area other than the corridors along Watkins and Danny Thomas. Whitehaven though it experiences white flight has survived much because middle class blacks refused to let it go under but it is a far cry from commercial and residential success. For those who don't know, Whitehaven is the home of Elvis Presley's Graceland and the corridor surrounding it has been approved for development that will hasten resurgence in the area that is much needed, perhaps mirroring the resurgence in Overton Square.

As this book will repeat as a common theme, poverty equals low education equals crime equals less desirable area, it's a circle really. You can easily switch the first two key words and argue that low education leads to poverty, they are arguably interchangeable. In a graduate studies class I had numerous African American counterparts say it is not really a matter of white flight but blight flight, I would agree with that situation more now, but in case of Whitehaven you would have to argue the former. Either way, the connections between ethnicity, movement of whites and money are closely connected and are making ways east across the city in a sort of convex curve or bow outwards. Memphis is bordered in the west by a large river most people know around the world-The Mighty Mississippi. The Mississippi River created a necessity for growth either north, south or east, but not west, which is the case for many cities forged near large bodies of water, a blessing and a curse. The stateline of Mississippi lies to the south of Memphis, to this day they touch, but in the 1960s, it was a much greater distance. Memphis has streets that many of them turn into highways, Stage, Poplar, Lamar, Jackson and so on, most of them run East and West. The North and South Streets of Third Street and Danny Thomas which link from the south and north ends of downtown did experience growth in the 50s and 60s as suburbs popped up; however, more growth was seen east towards Binghampton and Chickasaw Gardens.

From 1970 to this day most of the span of Memphis from midtown towards Germantown down the Walnut Grove and Poplar corridors has experienced little shift in demographics and so different ethnic groups have formed a stable symbiotic existence (which if looked at closely make up the most affluent areas in Memphis with exception to Binghampton), however the areas to the north and south have been met with sweeping change in demographics which has led to sprawl east in rapid form. Frayser started to slide into lower income and crime Raleigh just to the east experienced growth and influx. A mall was opened named the Raleigh Springs Mall which served as a shopping mecca for many in Memphis for years, the first mall in the US with 4 department stores. The same can be said for Southeast Memphis after Whitehaven experienced change, a mall was built called the Hickory Ridge Mall which also served many in Memphis. Downtown meanwhile didn't change much in demographics but fell into proverbial economic dark ages and then a renaissance in the later 1990s and early 2000s.

Consequently this pattern would not stop, and so, as Raleigh started to change, the mall went with it and Bartlett to the east would grow, though not a part of Memphis it was but a town until Memphians started pouring in from Raleigh and other urban sections of Memphis. Southeast Memphis would experience perhaps the most rapid change almost any urban area on record. In the 1990s, the area along Winchester west of Riverdale bled its influence into the more stable middle class Hickory Hill neighborhood. This influence would come in the forms of crime, noise pollution, gang activity of sorts all of which was on full display at the Hickory Ridge Mall nearby. Many Hickory Ridge residents went east or northeast into Cordova an unincorporated affordable area outside Memphis. Hickory Hill has not recovered except for the valiant efforts of local churches in restoring some semblance of community and solidarity, investing in the mall and providing services. If you have seen the trend you might like to guess which area you think would go next, Cordova, Bartlett, Germantown (an incorporated town north and east of Hickory Ridge), Collierville (just east of Germantown) or another? Well, in reading this, geographically Cordova or Bartlett by this equation would fall next.

One adage that has rung clearly with Memphians, if Memphis brings you in, get out, but the best proactive measure is to ask first: is this area incorporated? If yes, it's probably not going to change much the next 20 or 30 years, if no, then Memphis will usher in a new era. Cordova, once a bourgeoning suburb along Germantown

Road bordered by Bartlett in the north and Germantown in the south was next on the Memphis expansion list, and so after a seven-year court challenge for the right of Memphis to annex, portions of Cordova were annexed into the Memphis City Council Second District. These included the subdivisions and land developments of Countrywood (1995), Berryhill (1997), and South Cordova (2001). After several court and legislative challenges, Memphis completed its annexation of the Cordova region with the subdivision of Rockcreek, along U.S. 64 to the Fayette County line. Cordova is a more complex issue of contention since the writing is not as clearly on the wall for outsiders. Since the annexation, housing on average dropped in value over 50%, crime has risen and much of this attributed to the change from high ranked Shelby County Schools to poorly graded Memphis City Schools, which you will discover has a poor effect on the value or homes and demographics when they move in. As in most areas of the US at this time, Cordova has not fallen into apparent ruin because of its vast size and oversized inflated suburban housing market that has kept some solvency in the area. However the large apartment complexes that line the main corridor of Cordova not only bring questionable transient tenants but also crime.

Wolfchase Galleria hails as the newest installation of malls in Memphis, with exception to the outside shopping centers in Collierville and Southhaven, which I will get into later. Wolfchase has not held up to its potential because Cordova and Bartlett are shifting, the closest neighborhoods have changed demographics and thus the shopping patterns/tastes change. Consequently, because Bartlett has gradually changed making middle class whites uncomfortable, not so much due to crime but color or culture some have moved to Fayette County, Lakeland or Arlington to the east depending on what their financial options were.

So, you have a general layout of how the city of Memphis is doing, now quickly the towns outside of Memphis. Arlington to the east of Bartlett has an upper middle class base, safe from annexation and not likely to take on apartments which generally welcome lower income tenants into some areas with predominantly middle class residents, such was the fate of Cordova. Germantown and Collierville much older than the other surrounding towns were more adept to face challenges of sprawl with strict building codes, neighborhood regulations, and very high standards for planning. Hence, they did not make missteps other towns such as Cordova and Bartlett made. To this day, they remain crafty with what they approve and where giving developers a hard time for their "fascist" tastes. Southhaven and Olive Branch both to the south in Mississippi had alternate planning with differing affects. Olive Branch chose not to build in the city centre, nor allow excessive sprawl and had a more healthy reaction to the changes to the north, like a Germantown or Collierville keeping a small town ambience.

Southaven less watchful and careful with planning had a more Cordova-like manifestation along Goodman, traffic, apartments, too much shopping, but they made a careful choice in building an outside shopping mall. Wondering where I am going with this? The shopping area/mall is where the neighborhood converges, as goes the area, so goes the shopping. The shopping mall reflects the tendencies of the area, demographically, politically, economically ideologically and so on. If the shopping thrives, so the area thrives, if the shopping suffers so the area must be suffering. It is a measuring stick. The problem however is that when a shopping mall closes, the shoppers move east, into more stable areas. You might protest and say I believe in exclusion or elitism, but elitism is not a system purely coordinated by whites; other forms of filtering and intimidation can be applied. Noise pollution in cars, people walking in groups so as to run off the shoppers who want to shop, spend money, a menacing presence is a kind of elitism–and people feel uncomfortable. You say, it's their right, yes, but loitering doesn't help the economy nor keep stores, it's like crapping on your own lawn, eventually you don't want to walk in it anymore. Back to exclusion, today in Memphis, there are far more areas that a white couple would not want to enter than a black couple, is this organized intimidation or happenstance of a crime ridden area or something else?

When people come to a mall, do they travel in numbers, do they shop, do they loiter, is it cold in the winter there, what is the economic backdrop? These are elements to consider while considering approving a plan or developing a shopping area/mall. Raleigh Springs Mall is in ruin; Hickory Ridge Mall is hanging by a thread and the once celebrated and one of a kind mall (Memphians would say the best Memphis has ever had, an ice rink, far more space than Wolfchase Galleria etc.) the Mall of Memphis— fell quickly into ruin after several incidents of violence. The economic convergence in Memphis is falling on fewer and fewer places showing a scary forecast for more areas of Memphis. Downtown has survived, but is not an accurate reflection on the welfare of Memphis since a majority of tourist money flows into this region, Beale Street, The FedEx Forum, AutoZone Park and the Pyramid which is now being taken under the wings of Bass Pro Shop mislead visitors that the remainder of Memphis is fine and dandy, not so. There is potential, but it must be nurtured. Go East, stay off Poplar and go north or south from there and you will find a much different picture, not only of the economic status of Memphis but the cultural and social status that is ripping the fabric that makes the city great into shreds, so slowly people only notice when something horrific happens, more to come on that. Two towns that have cleverly avoided the mall slumps are Germantown and Collierville (Southaven to an extent) which have aired on the side of caution and allowed only outside shopping areas. What's with the outside shopping areas that work where inside doesn't?

Outside shopping areas have a connection to nature; this means in the winter it gets cold outside and in the summer very hot in Memphis—not for the climate sensitive or bourgeois to stay outside too long. This allows for little loitering or unwanted hanging out. The shops are not connected by hallways so you have to walk outside to shop, and sometimes walk a certain distance across a path to get a desired shop of your choice. What this continues to do is really test who wants to shop and who wants to just hang out, no teeny boppers or thugs here, that's really where the designers were going. Shops do have the increased proximity of workers and security cameras than to vast hallways with mall cops to watch suspicious behavior. Security outside the shops comes in the form of police or bikes or cars and so pursuit of shoplifters is even more efficient—if they chose to pursue. In some cases for the sake of preserving the image of safety some shops have been silent about theft and did not pursue the suspects. The themes of these out-door malls are also clearly small town ambience rather than cosmopolitan motif or avant-garde. The stores have a greater range of boutique and respectable chains rather than lower end stores that pepper Wolfchase, or even more so at Southland Mall (the oldest mall in Memphis—in Whitehaven), Raleigh Springs Mall and Hickory Ridge Mall. All of this combined and what you get is a prescription for more affluent buyers, white and black, stores that can stay open because people are generally buying and people feel safe. The large groups of loitering youth shy away from this environment. So you have recipe to avoid gang violence, people running off those who want to shop and risk of parking lot events that forced a local theater to make even stricter guidelines on whom and when someone can watch a movie. More on that issue later. If you understand, a place of public meeting is where the economic vibrancy or lack thereof is on full display and as with most large cities with closed malls, theaters, places of amusement reflect poorly on the area. People whether consciously or subconsciously use a shopping experience as a barometer for the conditions of the area. I just find it fascinating that those who contribute to the closing don't get it, or if they do their stupidity precedes them. Most civilized people enjoy clean public spaces, yet, they don't want to contribute to its cleanliness and so, people who do go elsewhere, the shops fail, and the shopping area looks dreary. So, those who ruined the last one go to where it's happening, only to ruin that place as well.

The problem in Memphis is its generally African Americans who are the culprits or that's general consensus: loud, obnoxious, uneducated (some however who are as well educated) mostly below forty who contribute to this detriment, and most older African Americans have said to me in discussion, it's embarrassing to them.

The black youths of Memphis are destroying the bridges that have been built by their predecessors and spitting on the graves of the countless generations of African Americans who sacrificed their livelihood for the civil rights and general livelihood of their children. The earlier chapter covered the inherent problems in rap, clothing styles and speech that are attributed to African American culture that has had a detrimental influence on blacks and whites and others. So, before you call me a racist, oh, too late—you might want to prepare yourself for some surprises in the next chapter.

chapter VII

A Personal Perspective

The mass of men lead lives of quiet desperation. ~Henry David
Thoreau, Walden

My life has a superb cast but I can't figure out the plot. ~Ashleigh
Brilliant

You can't escape history, or the needs and neuroses you've picked
up like layers and layers of tartar on your teeth. ~Charles Johnson

We are born wet, naked, and hungry. Then things get worse.
~Author Unknown

To explain myself further and perhaps help those curious who wonder why would I even right this book, this might help. I was born in 1979 in an area called midtown almost in the direct center of Memphis Tennessee. Midtown is known for its most diverse mix of cultures of African descent, European, Chinese, Mexican, Laotian, Puerto Rican and many others. It is also the oldest established residential area still remaining since the older downtown district is largely commercial now and has just more recently begun building condos and lofts to accommodate a youthful upper-middle class and retirees. A well-known section that includes a mélange of great restaurants is called Cooper Young, this anchors the southern end of midtown which ends at Southern. The Eastern edge is dominated by a shopping area called Poplar Plaza home to some restaurants like Buffalo Wild Wings and McAllister's, stores like Old Navy and don't forget Kroger. The University of Memphis falls just outside the perimeter a quarter-mile to the southeast across Highland. To the west is the Crosstown corridor that separates midtown from the medical center along Watkins and Cleveland. Central High, the oldest high school in Memphis lies here. This area is very diverse with shops for Vietnamese and Chinese food along with an international market. To the north is a largely residential dense labyrinth of housing interspersed with industrial warehouses along Chelsea. Polar, Madison and Union Avenues run through the core of Midtown going east and west while Cooper, McLean and Evergreen/Belvedere run north and south.

A large section of midtown is centered by Overton Park home of the Brooks Museum of Art, The Memphis College of Art, one of the finest in the US, and the Memphis Zoo, which has in the last 15 years, has worked to become one of the preeminent zoos in the world. There is also Rhodes College and the Vollintine Evergreen area, which in essence make up two of the staples of the midtown image. I grew up on North Belvedere, blocks away from Rhodes College and Overton Park and across the street from the park was my school—Snowden Middle School, where I attended for 8 years.

Much of my childhood was a peace filled upbringing on an all-white street, pristine with a beautiful canopy of trees amongst middle class housing, 3 bedroom 1 or 2 bath bungalows built in the 1920s. My mother Debbie was from a small town further north where she had a very-poor upbringing and so to her this was probably almost like a utopia, except when the monthly bills came around. My father grew up on Spottswood in an area known today as Orange Mound, but in his day it was a predominantly white neighborhood with large lots and lush greenery just blocks away from the most elite golf club in the mid-south town. With mainly reading, the sandbox and television as my friend, my sister and I sometimes played with friends down the street or rode our bikes in the safer areas, basically anything south of Jackson. One thing about the midtown experience, you will learn how quickly it can evolve and what areas are safe and which streets white people dare not travel except quickly in a vehicle or in large numbers, this sounds like an exaggeration, but isn't this the description of other urban areas around the country?

This is Memphis in the 1980s; midtown is but an area, but I later found out that it's an island. To the north and south from the river and going east, much of Memphis was changing around me, and not for the better in most cases, but I didn't see it that way. My limited interaction with people of color was about to change when my mother had to place me in public school in second grade. Much of my perception of black people was almost mythological. I once shook a black kids hand at the Raleigh Springs Mall and immediately looked to see how much of his color had rubbed onto my hand; I was 6 or 7 then. I attended a private school for preschool and kindergarten, all white from my recollection. My first grade was at an all-white school on Highland on the edge of Midtown called First Assembly Christian School, nothing but white as far as the eye could see from the drive in and when they picked me up. I was in my little bubble, the world around me was about the come breaking in. My mother was sending my sister then in the fourth grade and I to private school and it became apparent that the finances wouldn't allow us to stay there another year, time to let the tax money go to work. I did not see it coming, even though I have a clear remembrance of my mother telling me, with a certain level of calm and determination that I was going to encounter children with whom I had no apparent similarities except our age and basic physiology, that idea would change too.

Walking to school my first day was more exciting than terrifying, more terrifying was it for my parents later on while searching for various offices because of the vast size of the school. My second grade class comprised of about 30 students, 3 of which were white. I quickly befriended one of the white students, but was intrigued by one of the black girls, who I was what we would call infatuated. I had a black teacher, Mrs. Franklin, whom I fell in love with and who had an interest in me perhaps because I was such a daydreamer but well behaved. My experience in that class did not involve hanging out with students black or white off campus. Snowden was the extent of the interaction with people of any color, and seven hours of the day made quite an impression. My school life at Snowden in the second grade was nothing to formulate prejudice but rather friendship and impartiality. Outside my small scope around my house all of my other friends were at my church Merton Avenue Baptist where it was a totally detached. The church was all white, conservative, even isolated because its surrounding area was primarily black, Asian and Mexican with a few remaining whites who had bought a house in the Binghampton area years ago when it was entirely white. Binghampton was just several miles from the Vollintine Evergreen district and Snowden School. It was once a town autonomous from Memphis influence until it was incorporated following World War II and it slowly changed over the decades. Merton Avenue Baptist Church was a remnant of Binghampton's formerly middle class white past. One could say that Merton's membership in the 1980s was a snapshot of Binghampton in the 1950s.

For much of my life I would live a detached life between school and church, never did they intertwine concerning friendships, events or anything. At Merton I was a good Christian, memorizing Bible verses, learning hymns (my dad was the church organist, my mom sang in the choir) and whole kit and caboodle. At Snowden, I was the relatively quiet, adventurous, underachieving but respectful student. We looked the same, but in many cases we weren't the same people, but I never introspectively reflected that paradox until years later in High School. I was a good looking kid, modest, brown hair, brown eyes, average height, a little skinny—but good enough to get the attention of the scarcity of white girls there as well as some cute black girls. I remember their names quite vividly and as my fingers tap the letters to form this sentence I can recall on numerous occasions during my second grade rite of passage when the girls would give me little strip teases with their shirts and bras, I saw no color, just pretty girls. Oh to be 8 again. My entrance into the third grade and then the fourth would meet little fanfare. I did not excel in academics due to my learning disability whereby I could not understand a subject or idea by verbal instruction, I was a visual learner. I would not learn the tricks to get around this disability until years later, but it did make my daydreaming quite excessive and thorough. I had a white teacher in the third grade, Mrs. Harvey, and then Mrs. Jordan a black teacher in the fourth. It was almost like the district was trying to alternate the ethnicities of my educators to make me feel demographically balanced, but that was not to be.

In this school district there were clear demographic nuances that if you looked closely were very apparent. The Vollintine Evergreen and Evergreen Historic districts in the 1980s and still much today are ethnically and economically opposites. These two areas comprise the majority of Snowden students but rarely did they seen to intermingle. At Snowden you were either an optional student or a standard student, this was mostly apparent from K through 6 (now K-5). The majority of advanced/optional students were from affluent homes south of North Parkway with white skin and the standard students (including me) were on a lower income bracket north of the North Parkway and mostly had a darker tone of skin. These two groups did not seem to care the other existed even to the point at recess that we all kept to ourselves. In third grade when I moved from a portable to the oldest section of the building, I noticed this dichotomy from the very beginning. To be frank, I did not talk about it, but it bothered me, because I noticed that us standard students had our shortcomings, we weren't near the braggarts that the optional counterparts were. The third grade optional class had an awesome teacher who just happened to write the song "Here at Snowden" still sung today, that didn't help my envy-meter either. This time in my life I had the first epiphany that some people are born with it, and some without, and whites usually have it—it's just that my folks didn't. I had to tweak that vision of reality time and time again in the coming years, but much of it still stands. If affluent white people get offended by that, they shouldn't thank themselves, most wealth wasn't self-inflicted, they should thank some lucky precursor who didn't lose it in the crash of 1929 or get swindled out of a profitable land deal centuries ago in North Carolina like my predecessors.

You might sense some tension here, and, you may see where I am going, but most likely, you haven't pegged me, and you won't—I just hope to simplify the complexity that is my 33 years on this planet. My sense of confidence was derived from the extracurricular efforts I made at home and in various clubs. My mother and father allowed me to experiment in various extracurricular studies at the Memphis College of Art, Boy Scouts, the Memphis Boys Choir, and Karate. Each endeavor allowed me to get my feet wet and know what fitted me more. My father being an organist influenced me to go in the musical direction rather than taking other roads while I was learning about myself in elementary. Starting as early as age 7, I was the navigator for any vacationing or short trips my family made, really, I actually corrected my dad on occasion which way to go. My bedroom walls were adorned with maps, and so by extension I was more than familiar with the intricacies of mapping. Once again, my school, church and my home life did not intersect, if any did, home and church did because my mom invited ladies her age to the house, which I was actually excited when we played host. Fifth grade brought orthodontic work into my existence, my cool modest appeal started to slide, I was loosing what ambivalence I had amongst my darker melanin counterparts. Sixth grade brought suffering to my existence in the form of glasses. Little were my parents aware that it would shift my appearance but more importantly my image to girls. I didn't really care what guys thought deep down, I was a lone wolf, I didn't hang out with guys, I abhorred their jock and stench (so I called it) I liked girls—there were no illusions.

My world was splintering into more parts, extra-curricular, church, school and home. Each element has its own demographic makeup none alike and each with its own rules. While I was in the Memphis Boys Choir color didn't have any weight, I was amongst music lovers. Home was home, mom, dad and sis my new cocker spaniel Richie, just acquired. During the 8th grade I was privileged to have an American History teacher with a passion for maps and stories. The Civil War had always been a curiosity for me, but my 8th grade teacher, Mr. Lewis, opened up a whole new level of appreciation and love for history. Another interest flourished during my middle school years while I followed my father around the city on certain Sundays–architecture. Living in Midtown, I was in the best location to observe and learn more about historical architecture. Luckily architecture and history seem to go hand in hand.

One might wonder, which of the three interests would claim victory during High School–music. The actual deciding factor that led me to pursue music in High School was the necessity for a transfer. I was able to audition for the revered Overton High School Choir program many thanks to my middle school choir teacher, Mr. Hamilton. My next three years would be a greater influence on personal life and have a more positive affect than any other time in my 33 years, thus far. The choir program there was demanding and it pushed everyone to excellence, this is mainly due to the leadership of Dr. Lulah Hedgeman. Dr. Hedgeman could be responsible for many things that transpired later in my life because without her I would have been much more timid and apprehensive as I set my sights on college. She was awarded The National Teacher of the Year by Disney personally by Oprah and had many accolades making her essentially one of the preeminent teachers of high school choirs in the US in the 1980s and 1990s. She not only taught us the nature of music but of life and what to do with it and how to be the best in whatever you pursue. She deserves a biopic essentially so those who never came to see her would understand what made her special and how she impacted people around her. Her impact was epic in my life, she lit a fire in me.

The University of Tennessee was my next stop and my most enjoyable educational experience. Upon application, my intent was to join the school of architecture and stay for 5 years, be an apprentice and earn my license. After the first semester of getting to know architecture's unpleasant business demands, the artistic infatuation I had for the profession has diminished. Fortunately I had several other interests that I could declare in the second semester as a major: history. After three years in Knoxville, including one stop at the University of Wales, I was determined to find my way into a well-known program that focused on ancient Middle Eastern history. Little did I know that knowing only two languages set oneself way behind the curve of applicants. However, my plan B for attending Southwestern Baptist Theological Seminary was not deterred and I earned a Masters of Arts in lay ministry (likened to a MAPS) in two years while in Fort Worth.

My next plan was to return to Memphis and teach, but I did not have a license, and so to pay bills I worked at On the Border for about two years, then Office Max, I worked my way up to manager at Dominos and Ramp Agent at FedEx. Each position over those 4 years were disappointments but they gave me invaluable wisdom in management, working with people, planning and numerous other qualities that a teacher needs to succeed. I taught at Shadowlawn Middle School, a Shelby County School with an even mix of blacks and whites, for a year while I was honing my craft and making strides I started my book. Then I taught at a Memphis City School in Westwood for almost a year and decided to venture further into my writing and entrepreneurial work. Starting five years earlier I was doing landscaping part time, and realizing that I would not achieve my goals in writing I made landscaping my primary profession and have never been happier.

Between Seminary (2000) and marriage in 2007 I dated the whole rainbow of female human existence and I would wager every tax bracket. This set me up for learning that college would not afford me and give me an even wider appreciation for different ethnic groups, their idiosyncrasies and culture as a whole. At the end of that 7 year gauntlet where I want through the valley spiritually from light to darkness and back into light I found my wife from Kenya and just a year and some months later a beautiful daughter. Our marriage flies into the very face of racism and dares it. A southern middle class white boy from the south marries a black kikuyu Kenyan woman. Our marriage provides us with situations that explore cultural boundaries and norms every week. Out of these situations arise some friction and introspection, but out of it greater knowledge. We tango with these assumptions and ideas and articulate which is relevant and objective and usually come to some agreement, though as with any couple there are areas we don't discuss. Each day we find more refinement in our understanding of each other and our backgrounds and by extension our intersecting cultures. I would not trade it for the world and would wish only more people try it, because black is beautiful, white is beautiful but mixed is perfection.

chapter VIII

A Personal digression

If a white man falls off a chair drunk, it's just a drunk. If a Negro does, it's the whole damn Negro race. ~Bill Cosby

To live anywhere in the world today and be against equality because of race or color is like living in Alaska and being against snow. ~William Faulkner, Essays, Speeches and Public Letters

Before I finish this book with a positive closing chapter I must digress, what I have realized through reflection of both personal and public components is that everyone contains at least a grain of bigotry. Four years ago, as I started writing the closing section in my book Barrack Obama lays forth his blueprints to change America in his St. Paul Democratic nomination speech in 2008. I had hopes to publish in this book in the following months. Well, its 2012, that didn't happen. Ok, back to 2008: I surmise that most people are looking at his accomplishment as the first African American to go this far politically as a sign of progress. The notion that Obama's victory has suddenly caused the paradigm to shift and the doors of repression to blow open is a nice idea but naive. I thought as the crowd applauded, they don't see color do they. What a novel idea, to look at someone for the content of their character and not the color of their skin. Nevertheless, it actually looks like they want to listen to what he has to say, of course he has been running for 16 months now edging past Mrs. Clinton just as I write. Funny that I am not convinced that this is a sign of more change to come. Sure, what he has achieved breaks barriers that only after several months or years of retrospection will we be able to wrap our heads around. What I am proposing however is that at best his surge of civil rights progress is an aberration at best.

What I have observed from many people from the democratic persuasion is that he is an accomplished, eloquent and well-spoken politician. Many Americans however first hear his name which sounds neither black nor American. Second they notice that he has pigmentation much different than theirs. These people who will go nameless are not a minority and the first group that cheers with exuberance over his victory perhaps looks at the leader best suited over others. Ok, four years later: I see even more division and bigotry now because of his presidency. You know where people stand quick when his name is brought up. It's bigotry that stifles growth and clarity from whites and blacks on a national scale where they lose sight of what really needs to be done. One might argue though not directly his fault, Obama has polarized this nation more. This doesn't have to be black on white or Asian or any combination thereof, it can be cultural or economic bigotry. It's something imbedded in the psyche from childhood that emerges for most of us very seldom—but it acts through us subconsciously as an influence. Much the same way we all incorporate the characteristics of our environment, from home to street, from school to work—likewise we also assimilate into our being prejudices exposed to us at an early age. From there these ideas can evolve, but they are there—in one form or another. The wealthy are afforded them certain condescension's that ultimately manifest themselves in waves of falsehood (rarely in truth) for which we must all aspire to break. In turn, those without are bitter and justify actions unbecoming to any man.

Terms of agreeing to disagree or be free to express without genuine acceptance may have to suffice but a solution of tolerance has to be met nonetheless. There will be only further ethnic turmoil that manifests itself in school violence, riots, prejudicial politics and in due course citywide decay in Memphis and other major cities. For example, for the wealthy, philanthropy is often like political posturing by which a smoke screen covers the discomforts between the givers and receivers. Another would be the legal advantage most evidently displayed in the 1990s trials of several celebrities. Conversely, the poor are disadvantaged and are hard pressed to subsist on unequal playing fields so many of them commit crimes the wealthy would not seriously consider—often for money or goods, to pay for food or drugs. We are all prisoners in terms of financial subsistence for which class-ism is born. What man has made of his status has stirred the waters of history. In war and peace who we are and where we go in life rests very heavily of what we were born of, in color and standing. Historically ethnicity has not been of much consequence as religion and class have so violently and powerfully displayed in texts and other forms of communication. So it is confounding that something as shallow as color (philosophically insignificant and in the grand scheme superficial) has affected, rather crippled and polarized modern thought and history so thoroughly. Summarily we are all infuriated when, as Logan Pearsall Smith states, "he is forced to drag out his dark convictions!"

Subconsciously we either refuse to acknowledge it, simply concede it's there, or embrace it—which is exploited for ill use by Skinheads, the Klu Klux Klan and some would argue the Nation of Islam (not to be confused with Islam). If you dispute with the latter you must not have heard any Farrakhan speeches. An amusing contradiction made by practically all of us is in our daily lives. What many of us eat, for example Mexican food, whether Tex-Mex or another term (let's not lower ourselves in semantics)—many of Americans right now are apprehensive about illegal aliens, Mexican and other Latinos taking our jobs. Do you see the absurdity? Likewise, we should second guess eating Mexican (Hispanolization incurred Spanish food with Yucatan foods as well, what few people know is that they very identity of Spain was an merging of Iberian and North African cultures before the 10th century AD), studying Algebra or many subjects today because they were all extracted by Christian crusaders from Post Muhammad Arab culture dating back over one thousand years. Now after driving your vehicle picking your kid up from school or going to Mexican restaurant, would you curse the Iraqis or Saudis or Egyptians? So if someone hates African Americans, how can that same person jamming to 70s rock, or 50s bubblegum be in sound mind continue listening to that jungle music, as some have called it over two hundred years.

All of us should agree familiarity can breed contempt, Charles Curtis states, "There are only two ways to be quite unprejudiced and impartial. One is to be completely ignorant. The other is to be completely indifferent." Our prejudices are usually brought to the forefront when our peacefully little world is challenged either by white cops breaking down the wrong doors or a car being stolen by a guy with a different shade of skin. Our cages get rattled and so we expound abundant discourses to God, our friends and for some our enemies. When all is well on the countryside we go back to that happy place of tolerance, which is what many of us desire. Lastly, H. L. Mencken wrote, "One may no more live in the world without picking up the moral prejudices of the world than one will be able to go to hell without perspiring." This is no way a treatise on closing the doors of racism forever, rather my intensions were open to dirty closets and cellars on both sides—especially for white America and stare our hypocrisy in the face.

Hopefully this will open the tables of discussion more, maybe take away some curiosities about those uncomfortable silences when you are around people of different colors. What I most wanted to establish was that, conversely, against what many white and black leaders have stated—the healing has not begun, we have only done a shoddy job of stitching up the wound with deceit or half-truths. An Assyrian proverb states: "time wounds all heals." In time, the bandage will be pulled back to reveal an infection. We have to put all our differences out in the open, at proper venues and diplomatically negotiate and ask questions, ask forgiveness, look to ourselves and move on. Otherwise, our escapism, whether geographical or psychological will be the end of America in more ways than we can envision.

The discord I have discussed thoroughly affects our city economically and its growth holistically. Both ends of the socio-economic spectrum need each other. From a business lens, a perfect capitalist example is the need for the US to have the third world supply raw materials and goods from places like Malaysia, China, and so on. The lack of a quality blue collar workforce severely cripples the local infrastructure and in the end the white collar jobs because their offices might need to move or downsize the basic ebb and flow of services from restaurants to shops will reflect poorly on the city of Memphis and scare off residents and tourists. The cityscape cannot continue to decay and push the affluent fringes further, there is a point when the deterioration has gone too far. Another element or many that will be discussed much more in the next chapter.

chapter IX

A glimpse of hope

Action and reaction, ebb and flow, trial and error, change - this is the rhythm of living. Out of our over-confidence, fear; out of our fear, clearer vision, fresh hope. And out of hope, progress. ~ Bruce Barton

We must accept finite disappointment, but never lose infinite hope. ~ Martin Luther King, Jr.

Leadership is the capacity to translate vision into reality. ~ Warren G. Bennis

In 2008 the mayor who ruled over Memphis for many years Willie Herenton left and Mayor Wharton has come onto the scene. I heard something that struck me and put a smile on my face. Mayor Wharton pronounces that whatever is going on in inner Memphis affects outer Memphis—too true, sadly many Memphians have an escapist perspective. This is not to attack those who had no other economic means or grew up solely in the outlying towns or moved to Memphis from another place unbeknownst to them the under-lying repercussions. Not in the sense that they just want a better life in the suburbs but that staying out of the hood and keeping a safe distance or rather ahead of the curve isn't the solution. What curve I am referring to has to do with the geographical curiosity that is Memphis itself. People over the last 60 years have steadily moved east in a sort of curved shape, with exception to what I called the Poplar Walnut Grove corridor. People who reside in this area are generally regarded as the wealthiest in Memphis, more so than those in Germantown or Arlington. Houses vary in size but usually cost well above the median housing price in Memphis, some may say that doesn't take much. Wharton wants to bridge the gap, literally and figuratively—this effort is taking form in many ways, but I will keep you guessing and we can cover that later in this chapter. Another good note: Tennessee Governor Bill Haslam has shown great interest in Memphis much more than his prede-cessors as governor.

Currently on my street in Midtown we have a gang activity problem as well as code violators who just make out street look less inviting and to be frank blighted. My neighbors who are pre-dominantly black agree with my assessment and just recently had an ad hoc meeting on the street just the three of us about the state of our street. We had a passionate discussion about how a group called the posse (an outcrop of the bloods) hold their influence between University and Watkins mainly using our street as a launching point or base for drug activity. Several houses on the street are in bed with this operation and either house drug dealers or assist them in some form such as out-lookers or just for appearance to make the dealers look more like visitors. This irritates me most because I know that five years ago when I left my house and came back an hour later my house was burglarized. This timing was curious and later came to find that residents on my very street collaborate on a daily basis with criminals. Detestable as it was and still is—this is the state of our city in many areas. Not everyone giving it 100 percent to rid their streets of lawbreakers because of complacency or a disregard for the future of their children is one of many reasons Memphis is clearly not winning the fight, because the fight cannot be won by police or legislation but a tri-pod effort, to stand together. So, as I and two of my neighbors stood outside for about 45 minutes and contemplated over what could be done, I proposed a simple structure that would not involve complex governance. I would type a cover letter explaining this survey that a neighbor drafted explaining the serious and timely nature of the content and explained that is the neighborhood around you deteriorates then your property looses too, safety is not there and you are really losing money. Along the way I proposed that we didn't need a president but just a group of people who call on issues of suspicious activity or code violations, three per category. I jested that I didn't mind seeing a cop car down the street on occasion because it would probably scare off activity for a short time. Here is what the cover letter looked like:

Dear Residents,

At this current time we are trying to organize or gather together people of like-minded views. Most people who have lived here for a short time or a long time have a general agreement that this street should maintain its safety and value in the greater area of VECA. Due to drug activity, code violations and other issues that have raised concern we are trying to gather information and find an agreeable time for residents to meet on occasion to discuss how we can better serve this street and ourselves. As most of you may know drug activity, constant loitering of cars on the street (suspicious traffic), excessive noise, and unkempt properties all lower the value of the houses around them. Your house is only as safe or as valuable as your neighbor's property. Property assessment depends highly on the appearance or image of the street on which the house resides. If the residents can come to agreements on how to make sure codes are enforced and watch out for suspicious behavior the likelihood of crime occurring is greatly reduced. The less crime, the higher the property value and this benefits our street in countless ways. If you could fill out the bottom of this sheet and take a few moments to fill out the other sheet we would be able to quickly address the issues discussed. <u>Please turn this in to the VECA office at the corner of Jackson and Belvedere.</u>

Concerning meeting at the VECA office:

1st What day(s) of the week could you meet (please circle the 3 days that are best for you)?

Monday Tuesday Wednesday Thursday Friday Saturday Sunday

2nd What time(s) of the day are you available (please circle the 3 best time slots)?

8am - 9am	11am - 12noon	2pm - 3pm	5pm - 6pm
9am - 10am	12pm - 1pm	3pm - 4pm	6pm - 7pm
10am - 11am	1pm - 2pm	4pm - 5pm	7pm – 8pm

3rd How frequently would you like to meet?

twice a month	every other month (6 times a year)
once a month	every three months (4 times a year)

A neighbor liked the directness of the letter and the length. I hope that while you read this you have formed a kind of appreciation for the forthcoming timbre of my writing and that my stance doesn't come from a place of color but respect for humanity and rights of those who respect others and law.

Now that you might have ascertained by now, several efforts have been made to link areas of Memphis figuratively and literally. One of them is a greenway that is linking the fairgrounds to Cordova in a 14 mile bike/walk trail that endorses healthy living, environmental conservancy and communal solidarity. More of this is to be explained in the following paragraphs.

Unlike politicians I don't have a 12 step or 5 step save the world program but rather a list of suggestions that can be altered to fit the exact needs of the city when the time comes that people start reading this book. Needs may alter but those I list here at the present time must be addressed with expeditiousness. Forgive me if there seems to be redundancy or overlap it really based on the necessity to reiterate certain concepts in my plan that most leaders are not fully seeing. It's a big picture problem and the leaders are not connecting the dots and if they are they are not saying it. One most pressing problem is the lack of leadership at our airport which is steadily regressing from international to regional. We need to clean house at the Memphis International Airport/ Airport Authority leadership level. The airport is a gateway to the nation and the world, we are isolated culturally, geographically and in commerce due to missteps by our leaders. Representative Steve Cohen has taken initiative to address the abuse by Delta Airlines and broken promises that have had negative consequences on the prices at the Memphis Airport, other airlines coming to Memphis and operations. A group on Facebook named Delta Does Memphis discuses daily the annals of ineptitude by Airport leadership and other disturbing elements that clearly show most in charge do not fully comprehend the major importance of a good airport in the grand scheme of city health. The mismanagement by the Airport Authority is appalling and if without revealing my sources I could bullet point the idiocy of their ways.

For just an example or two, the trees planted along the runways have attracted birds that nest and damage the aircraft on a weekly basis, but the management thought the birds would know better since they did not plant canopy trees. Another illustration is the relationship with Delta where we have let small businesses that cater to the airport be bullied and fallen into bankruptcy, airlines/ customers sustain astronomical airport fees, Pinnacle run out of town and Delta have the red carpet only to leave with our airport in ruin. We are not a destination airport and the aerotropolis distinction given Memphis Airport is a ruse and misleading at best. Ask them why the new tower was actually built, and how much some signs have cost that cannot be read but a local friend still gets the lucrative contract. Too much power and influence is given FedEx, a company that can move their operations to Indianapolis with a stronger more educated labor base, modernized, automated, efficient, and ready to accept the traffic that our city claims. The truth is, the cogged wheel concept is no longer active and Indianapolis is the second largest as a close second hub for FedEx, let us not be deceived like in times past that Memphis is safe, we are too sure of ourselves and ignorant of our city's past. The Airport Authority has let FedEx make deals most airports would be considered most unwise to grant. We still will have even with positive traction of US Air or Southwest or (fill in the space) have complete idiots running the Airport that do not have the professional capacity or ethical disposition to do the right thing. They will allow Southwest to become the new Delta, give FedEx the moon, abuse local small business, charge fees and have practices not conducive to having an efficient international Airport. They need to go, everything else happening at the airport is just window dressing or moot.

Against the recommendations by some of my esteemed economist friends and business associates I have seen that there is a need to seriously push forward a light rail or elevated train. Dallas, St Louis and Atlanta all have operating rail, and Nashville which has passed us by since the 1990s is in the process of expanding their mass transit infrastructure. MATA busses and the downtown trolley should complement the rail like other major cities, and the use of rail would connect less developed areas along the way between the outlying boroughs/towns and downtown. There are existing paths in place for rail that would provide three main paths that go through south Memphis, north Memphis and along the Mississippi north to south. Rail would connect the airport to downtown where there is a lacking a good connection for business travelers and tourists who don't want to make the questionable drive from the airport to downtown via rental car.

When we have a nationally (not just ok for the south) respected school system (not just a few schools getting merit badges) then we draw in families with the means to move come here with their jobs, ideas, money and more. Oh, and by the way, when you have strong education, you have lower poverty and lower crime. Let's not just throw 20 year old teachers and money at the problem, that's a bandage on a mortar wound. Let's rethink the process. It's the same leadership different name. Embrace the towns in the county and let them have their own school system, it's not racially driven although it can be argued that it's culturally driven, but cannot blame them. When Memphis acquires an area it's like the plague waltzed in, much the same way MCS has done with Shelby County Schools. There is another book entitled *The Education Artifice* which will detail the errors our education leaders are making amongst other national educational issues not tackled yet in a book. The methodologies by leadership in the new system being forged is like building a castle on sand, pouring federal money into new facilities and new teacher through various programs used nationwide. It's a system problem not simply a facility or motivated teacher problem, it is shown that traditional schools do not perform well in underprivileged areas regardless of the new building and fresh faculties handpicked from other schools. Yet, charter and other formats are not being pursued aggressively. This is a book in itself and will come with a minefield of problems if only grazed by a single paragraph, however, the need to totally rethink Memphis education is needed and we don't need County leadership forced into the merged system that are cringing at the thought of it and City School leadership in the merger thinking they got something to offer because both groups will fail in doing so. This is a slowly sinking ship and the captain is unaware that they are taking on water.

A list of high performing schools can be marked on a map with arrows. The highest performing schools (to some the previous school system) at Memphis City Schools are spread out. All schools doing well within the loop are traditional schools (non-charter, except Middle College on Central and East Parkway) and compete with the best Shelby County Schools. All of the schools outside the loop compete with SCS as well but are nontraditional and would suggest that traditional doesn't work in low income areas. We would show the low performing schools but it would appear as if a hail of arrows attacked the city. Plainly put: the average score for MCS: 4, the average score for SCS: 9. So the potential for inner city/low income/high crime students to excel is high, we just have to restructure the method.

The lowest performing Shelby County Schools received poor marks from multiple sources. There are some gaps, for example Cordova doesn't have as high a crime rate, but the housing prices are falling steadily and there are large numbers of apartments linked to lower income families which also coincides with crime over a period of time. Where am I going with this? No matter what school system, if you are running a purely traditional school format (95% of SCS) in a high crime or low income environment, your schools do not perform well. There are many facets involved in this, including core family structure (or lack thereof), parents with financial stability (or lack thereof) and more that will be discussed in detail in the next book of education.

There is a great need to stop putting bandages on the economy by celebrating a few hundred jobs. Even if those jobs equate to a few hundred families being affected. Our two biggest employers are a merged school system and FedEx, both have massive turnover (yes, the FedEx Hub too) and service all strata of tax brackets, so there is much more to be done to secure more industry. Too much influence is given to FedEx in the scheme of development around the airport and citywide. There is a big problem when your second largest employer is a school system, where do these high school grads go? All of these areas interconnect and do not organically change in a vacuum. So why are our local governing bodies structured in such a way as to suggest the opposite is occurring. Like a table that needs all of its legs, if we don't solidify the transportation infrastructure (airport, rail), commerce (jobs, new industry) and education (totally revamp) then the table will fall, I am not seeing the urgency from any leader locally to connect the dots and get Memphis into the 21st century with clear plan ala state of the union. Let's consider this truth, when people have jobs, people don't economically suffer the same as before. When people do not suffer economically, crime is reduced exponentially. Poverty, crime, lack of good education and unemployment are in the same race. When people see reduction in crime and have money as well, the city has an increase in attendance at events and can function at a higher level and grow. People don't come to downtown or midtown with money from the suburbs or the world outside unless they are at ease. This helps the private industry and public run venues. When people have jobs, crime is reduced, the city benefits in commerce from within and from without with industry coming here thus creating more jobs. This is a chicken and the egg argument that won't end, the point is, bring commerce, revamp the schools, and improve the transportation infrastructure simultaneously. When there are jobs here, a booming inner city, lower crime = people will be drawn to Memphis.

Industries are attracted by a strong educated labor base, we have lost that. Also, white collar executives want to send their corporate workers to cities with a strong public education system. Downtown benefits from all of this, so let's give people living in Memphis and visiting a glorious site to see downtown overlooking the river, so let's do more than Beale Street Landing, let's face the river with restaurants and shops. San Antonio has figured this out, why can't we? Chattanooga has done a lovely job of this, and yes, we have a river that rises and falls at great intervals, so that's why get people who protest the development of the promenade and explain to them that developing doesn't mean destroying. This city has shot itself in the foot historically too many times by people having idyllic intentions but ultimately destroying the potential for growth. Peabody Place is mothballed and is not being properly developed by the Belz family.

Ok, now that we have green friendly connectivity on the rise for all of our new residents from around the world who are just as familiar with biking and jogging. Let's connect tourist and Memphians to the Airport, and to the outlying suburbs. A light rail is more functional to a much greater percentage of people (obviously tourists and Memphians). This is all economically viable and possible, within a short period of time.

So, let's make sure our great neighborhoods are commercially viable and not alone, we need to connect them via a network more modern and efficient than MATA which to most 21st century cities would be not more than a compliment to the rail or elevated. We don't want our great neighborhoods to be islands of prosperity. Much the same way the train meant survival for a town in the old west, a transportation system that brings tourists and Memphians to each neighborhood brings more prosperity and growth and avoids blight and the dead neighborhood syndrome. We need a connected city, not a city of division and segmentation. Blight/white flight is a common discussion, but many things discussed are either unfounded or misunderstood. Crime, education and even the tourism industry are connected. It is good to ask questions yourself about what is often not told correctly by our local media (TV, paper etc.) and make up your own mind by seeing things objectively.

To most any human being on Earth, the picture of blight moving through the city of Memphis might seem like wind patterns. To most Memphians, depending on the demography of the person, it's either flight or the spread of crime and blight, but either way it's connected. One is the Lion, the other is the gazelle. If you simply Google crime rates in Memphis you will find maps all crime is considered and calculated into colors. If you are a dark shade of blue you are safe, when you start turning pale, it's not a good thing.

Memphians who actually know Memphis will say that you can't go by zip code or neighborhood necessarily when buying a house and you have to take it street by street. This is actually very true, one great neighborhood can have weaknesses on its edges. It's not like a castle with walls, you have democracy in action and people who can buy will buy and so crime follows the same approach. Midtown, isn't it just like an island? Where you see the yellow square its darkest blue underneath, curious that Collierville and Germantown have the exact the same color. By the way, follow Poplar and the Walnut Grove corridor and you are safe to buy a home and for public school as well.

According to Trip Advisor and other sources, they indicate the top tourist attractions in Memphis. There is a heavy concentration in downtown and Midtown, and with the exception of Dixon Gallery and Gardens and Graceland, you are within reach of most great attractions if you live in for example Cooper Young or VECA. Where am I going with this? Do tourists hear about Memphis before they visit, or do they suddenly show up and check it out at random. Media, family members, social sites all propagate the myth that Midtown and downtown are dangerous and this gets spread. All great cities have the same buffet of crime, poverty, wealthy and places to see, yet people can't stop running further away. Is it all justified flight? some of it, if you want a large home with and good public schools with a decent price tag, yes, going East is a reasonable tactic. Blight must be fought as well, even if from a defensive stance in a town. We don't have enough hotel rooms for large conventions (not for today's volume) why not have more around Overton Square where there was once a decent hotel? Why not have more large hotels near downtown as well since we want to draw more people here (tourists, business men and women, developers), we have to put them somewhere, right? So, don't forget as you spread the word about Memphis, sprinkle in some truth from time to time.

Hypothetically, let's say we link that previous trolley line all the way to Overton Square, then it is an automatic connection to Downtown and the booming South Main district. So, you connect two booming business districts that are growing exponentially in restaurants, shops, condos and offices. What a novel idea! Some of you may recognize this, it's a relatively seldom used venue for ceremonies and used only at two peak times (on average before midnight and early morning around 6am) for trains connecting with New Orleans, St Louis and beyond: Memphis Central Station. Tourists by the way statistically don't use buses except as a support system (connecting paths) to a larger umbrella system like rail or elevated train. This rail would be a logical connection to the airport, whereby people can connect to downtown hotels via the main street trolley or a more modernized transport for specifically hotel connections and the rail vice versa would lead people back to the Airport without having to brave the interstate and questionable streets along the way. Let's be honest, many airports have a better view to their city centre, let us also be considerate of tourists and business men and women who want to see the best in Memphis whether Graceland, South Main or Midtowns buffet of neighborhoods.

This is driving north on South Main, we have to be sure to not abandon South Main with a gap between them and the Orpheum, because the Belz family cannot be relied on. The lack of transparency concerning Peabody Place is a lesson in itself. Much like Charleston, Austin and San Diego who have a myriad of areas that connect via a transport system more modern than ours, you can see the cities without really needing a car. Fewer cars, less parking spaces filled, less pollution, and more. Bike lanes are great, but tourists don't spend their money riding around on bikes. Let's have a modern system, and trails and bike lanes.

You have people parking in lots who need to commute from their house, or tourists who want to actually see the city rather than brave the bad drivers here with their rentals. These trains connect the airport to the hotels, the hotels to the restaurants and shops, museums and so on. Oh and maybe even a water park someday, but somewhere with space, not like Libertyland with its limited vision and most importantly limited land. Today's city planners are much like the planners in the 50s and 70s and other decades who build something with limited insight and vision and often with an ill-fated result because they don't know the basics. Like for example, a basic amusement or theme park would require space (100 acres is a good start though many range from 200 to 25,000 acres), hotels for tourists nearby and ambitious situational awareness for what sells (roller coasters, shows which needs money, which requires people). Let it be noted this is not an attack on the management of it, nor the great local support, but the foundational issues like where it was placed regardless of the history with the Pippin, just move it. Let's not build a Libertyland, let's build something greater. You can apply this to the under-conceived Cannon Center and the new MATA bus they are trying to introduce that is a more affordable option than a light rail transit which is far superior. This analogy applies to transportation, waterparks, and all sorts of venues. Connect the dots, see the whole canvas where our predecessors did not.

You change the city locally before you start using broad strokes across the cityscape. Here is an example where it has worked. We want to propose that the latter is the best option for connecting the city, instilling a competitive and supportive infrastructure for commercial growth, residential improvements and family friendly neighborhoods. At the Overton Park Shell people will pour in from all directions to see various shows and events, but the range in each direction could possibly grow, if each community would reach out to another with various events. On High Point Terrace there is the High Point commercial core which has experienced a new rush of businesses and good traffic the last five years. It is a gem of a place and could grow more. Cooper Young, perhaps the most accomplished of Neighborhood Associations with the best street festival in town and the best buffet of restaurant venues in all of Shelby County. There are several business districts in VECA and will hopefully be accompanied by several more places of interest in VECA along McLean, Jackson and Vollintine in the near future. The Broad Avenue Arts District is a quickly growing neighborhood or rather business district by which locals brought a single street to life. Ten years ago the sight of it was not feasible except for the imaginations of a few. Every neighborhood has a gem that locals flock to ice cream parlors on a hot summer's day. The network we are proposing would benefit all parties (neighborhoods) involved and spur growth on a commercial and residential front. Also, create a more family friendly ecosystem.

It has been said to me as a citizen that I was too harsh at calling Memphians apathetic to crime and blight. One is married to the other, yet, many who stay in inner cities are lax at attacking crime and blight and hitting it where it hurts. It's hypocritical to call sub-urbanites escapists when their actions were although multifaceted (some good and some bad motivations) were sincere and with certain upsides. However, among my inner city brethren, there is division in the ranks as to how should we move forward and bring Memphis into the 21st century and put crime, blight and all other undesirables in their place. Concerning that very idea, there is division altogether if we want to get rid of crime and blight at all. This may sound absurd, but the actions of leadership on a local level and citywide raise that very question. I am hopefully shedding light on the mechanisms of crime and how it negatively affects a city on many levels that you might now consider a city is comprised of many neighborhoods operating like independent ecosystems though tied through various government entities and local organizations that make a modern city tick. Most of us have had science. The term ecosystem is defined as a community of living organisms (plants, animals and microbes) in conjunction with the nonliving components of their environment (things like air, water and mineral soil), interacting as a system. You can insert other words to describe a neighborhood. In every thriving neighborhood there is a commercial backbone, though varying in size and overall impact citywide, this commercial district or districts is a barometer for the neighborhood and how it is doing in other areas. Plainly put, if you have restaurants and/or shops that look pre-sentable and occupied during business hours then the surrounding neighborhood is probably healthy as well. A healthy neighborhood is communal as well, children feel free to congregate and mingle. It is a haven for activities and displays a vibrancy that can only be reflected most accurately by the interaction of children and the assurance of the parents that all is safe.

Crime is inevitable. The frequency of it is the key. Every town has a homicide, if it is a common occurrence, this is a clear marker of familial strife and deterioration of the neighborhood itself. The key is: keep crime at bay. Crime rarely stops, it usually migrates. This is where concerned citizens must step up to the plate and hit it out of the park; don't just bunt the ball. It is most important at the sign of a crime wave or questionable activity to be vigilant and proactive. Do not expect conventionally accepted practices of police to suffice, they need your help. Keep a sharp eye and do not let your household be bullied on a street you call home.

The legalization of drugs (although there are many clever arguments concerning just that) is one delicate topic although reasonable if limited to certain drugs and treated like prohibition. Nevertheless, the baggage that comes with the trade itself in a residential ecosystem is undeniably corrosive. It is detrimental to the fabric of what we discussed earlier about commerce and safety for children that most people don't get. There is a link between the sale of drugs and the downfall of a neighborhood. For that matter, all crime, once it is accepted by a community as simply part of the package then that neighborhood will slowly or rapidly deteriorate. The greater the apathy by citizens and the leadership the quicker the descent. Do not rely of politicians to save a community, often they will use crime and blight as a sounding board for their own political gain. If they were truly effective, many would have to find new ways of stirring the local electorate. It is also a battle won locally street by street, don't assume the neighborhood association can do it alone, there needs to be a real, innovative and expeditious approach to solving what ails the community.

This is a byproduct of a deteriorating community. The lack of leadership and a street level cohesive front against crime and blight will lead to a domino effect slope of house prices (the economy is rarely the culprit) and ultimately bring in a new tax bracket to the community that people find out later is most unwelcome. As a community falls, so do the schools that are linked to it. So, if you have remotely high standards for your child's education, you are more likely to send your children to private schools when living in a neighborhood on the decline. It's bad business to allow crime to subsist. It angers me when neighborhood leaders say it's great to have affordable housing. When such a statement is made, in light that the housing prices were competitive and reflecting better on the quality of the community, it is really a statement of ignorance. There are real consequences for a neighborhood when houses once worth 300,000 now suddenly are 150,000. This will cause people of lesser means who have a variety of motivations (some good, some bad) to move into your neighborhood and ultimately bring down the image and quality of your community. This is not about diversity, Midtown has experienced integration for decades, but only more recently has shown sides of decay on its fringes and in pockets where housing has become rent, drug dealing and prostitution are midday operations and blight has crept in at an alarming rate. This is much to blame on the lack of action by neighborhood citizenry essentiality asleep at the wheel. This is not a matter simply to be dumped on a local association for salvation, but a matter to be aggressively remedied by neighbors. Remember, rampant crime in your vicinity really means your house is worth less and your insurance is more, think about it!

Another byproduct of a deteriorating neighborhood is lower taxes on the home. Sadly, many people will look at this as a plus, but in their limited vision don't realize it is a curse in disguise because it simply means your home is worth less. In a selfish way, parents who don't care if their children inherit good property or not think along the same lines. Yes, subsistence is great for your generation, but it is in the best interest of our future to leave the world a better place and to move our offspring into a higher tax bracket if at all possible or more independence from government involvement or banks. People that quote, money can't buy you happiness didn't either have money or didn't know what to do with it. Having a property that is in a vibrant neighborhood to hand down to a child or grandchild is a great thing.

If one doesn't show great concern for the little things creeping in like a less than aesthetically pleasing landscape (code violations friendly to rat infestation), or a curious fellow with a penchant for drug trading, or a car driving aimlessly through a neighborhood as if scouting then you might as well join the people in the burbs. It's about taking action, working with police, and the street as a collective to have an action plan to stop crime, prevent further blight and to look optimistically into the future since you are all the captain of your fate.

A Conclusion

As for the "Master Plans for Memphis" how much is fact and how much is fiction? Mark Twain once said, "there are lies, there are damn lies, and there are statistics" I wish to change the ending with "and there are Master Plans" Growing up in Memphis seeing Snowden School's Master Plan and Bellevue Baptist's never fully come to fruition, I have reservations. Renderings are often the optimistic end result with a glossy facade, but often what you get is half of that. It is not a malicious process (with exception to the FedEx Forum) but usually just what happens when budget constraints and other elements settle in. Keeping a grounded understanding in the mechanism of grand ideas coming to fruition will allow you to better prepare.

A good architect whether he favors form or function more will always tell you that planning is the most important aspect of the whole process. While planning, do not hasten nor tarry but keep a steady pace that will ensure confidence in leadership and not force those foreign to your vision into a corner. It is imperative that leaders for the sake of progress take off the robes of partisanship and project a vision that is clear and direct. To paraphrase Augustine, speak plainly so that you may be understood. Transparency is key, a website that clearly states the findings of statisticians and lays out a game plan for the future of our city is needed. A website that is not laborious to read and is easily navigable and comprehensive should be designed and launched. It is of course in the nature of deliberation to use discourse and public speaking like playing chess and allowing bids and agreements to take proper form as leaders. However, it is upon the citizen of Memphis to vote with their ideas and not allow nepotism, repeated failures or same old same old to thrive. The citizens must not allow poor leadership to continue but leadership must do their part to avoid city polarization and segmentation.

Other factors that held Memphis back and zapped wealth from the city over one hundred years ago were two outbreaks of the Yellow Fever, the wealthy and other socially mobile left and this allowed surrounding cities in the south like Atlanta and Nashville (who we know now have surpassed Memphis by most standards) to bounce back that had suffered under northern union army campaigns during the Civil War. Politicians like Boss Crump held Memphis back by isolating it from Tennessee, being a bully and tyrant to many though glorified locally for his efforts to provide jobs through projects and but giving us the red headed step child complex. We were not in favor in the capital for many decades and some of it still shows to this day where a majority of Tennessee doesn't look with much admiration on Memphis. Wherever your governor calls home, that area will show more industrial development, better roads, better funding for schools and various public projects. People throughout the world admire Memphis for the blues, Elvis, Sun Studio, STAX, Shelby Farms, the green spaces and canopy of trees, the arts and more but the state in which Memphis resides has for decades not allowed funding and other proposals to go through such as horse racing in the 1920s, thus crippling efforts to thrive economically and by extension most every other way. Memphis needs to make efforts to save the image it has, like solving the municipal school circumstance with more ease and less polarizing monologues. The decision by the judge to not allow further progress on municipal school organization will push many people into private school decisions, some may just move, others will trudge onward and form their own district in the coming years. The exodus from Memphis will continue much of it because of poor public education, crime on the rise, lack of jobs and the areas we have discussed in great need of attention. They all inter-relate. It is inevitable and Constitutionally sound for local towns to form their own school systems regardless of the motivations, some with purely good incentives, some mixed, some not pure. The residents of Memphis must understand that Memphis needs the outlying towns for their services, local ownership, the commerce and taxes. It's a marriage and we need each other. Essentially Memphis like all metropolitan areas exist in an ecosystem of urban and suburban worlds and must coexist with a sense of balance in commerce, education, tourism, industry, and more. However, Memphis the balance is awry and in need of reform simultaneously without political bias and with expediency. Consequently the equation of diversity that makes our music and art community so rich is also in the center of the storm of cultural and ethnic warfare from people who do not realize wealth of talent that has made Memphis the epicenter of stars for nearly a century relies on this diverse pot-pourri that is distinct to the fabric of Memphis.

Much of what historically has held Memphis back is self-inflicted from the upper classes down to the lower classes and then back. White Mid-Southerners who look with disgust at the state of Memphis and the blight should only thank in part their ancestors for laying the stage that created the state of lower income Americans in the Delta. Outspoken racists are most hypocritical because their practices and those of their predecessors ran the plantations or were complicit, didn't adapt to industrial change, started hate groups, enforced Jim Crow, held back African American progress, fought against Civil Rights initiatives like integration where they could have simply given equal opportunity and access for all thus possibly avoiding integration which they despised the most. It's likened to a chef of a banquet preparing a whole feast over many hours and then because he doesn't like the outcome then blaming the food. White supremacists are the most contradicted and historically ignorant of them all, not realizing cause and effect, action and reaction.

This is not to imply that white Memphians and those in outlying areas are racists, because racism, ethnicism or culturalism (those last two I just made up) as might be more accurate titles comes in shades like blue comes in many forms. The most common group would likely be on the side of apathetic/indifferent white Memphian but not definitive bigot. There would be no study to confirm or survey to illuminate this conundrum because the questionable transparency or anonymity in the process would not give exact results and to think otherwise is folly. Consequently many people without and within the confines of the city limits have varying conflictions on the segmented state of the Memphis Metropolitan complex, the perception of responsibility, their own beliefs of their open mindedness or lack thereof. Example: many educated inner city whites call suburbanites cop outs, in so many words, it is usually not blacks who blame the suburbanites for their stance. We have more private support and state level support in recent years and it seems that local leadership is taking advantage of it, however still not creating self-reliant lines of revenue, our city relies too much on the generosity of other people and companies. There are not clear lines of good and bad, it is a matter of simply starting where we are and moving forward with an understanding of what made Memphis what it is still conducts the cities future. It is an underlying but apparent state of reality that we are a city of diversity and division, like a mosaic we must make a complete picture together.

Notes

Notes

Notes

www.ingramcontent.com/pod-product-compliance
Lightning Source LLC
Chambersburg PA
CBHW020506030426
42337CB00011B/255